RESEARCH PAPERS

Sixth Edition

William Coyle

Professor of English
Florida Atlantic University
Boca Raton, Florida

Macmillan Publishing Company
New York
Collier Macmillan Publishers
London

Macmillan Publishing Company
866 Third Avenue
New York, New York 10022

Sixth Edition 1984
Third Printing — 1987

Acquisition and Development: Paul O'Connell
Editorial Production/Interior Design: Sara Bernhardt Black
Cover Design: Kevin Caddell
Composition: Compolith Graphics
Printing: Howard W. Sams, A Division of Macmillan, Inc.

Library of Congress Cataloging in Publication Data

Coyle, William.
    Research papers.

    Includes index.
    1. Report writing.   2. Research.   3. Title.
LB2369.C65   1985   808'.02   84-6423
ISBN 0-02-325360-6

RESEARCH PAPERS
CONTENTS

INTRODUCTION

Few moments are more pleasing than those in which the mind is concerting measures for a new undertaking.

TO THE INSTRUCTOR

This manual is designed to guide a student in preparing a research paper for a freshman composition course and for other college courses. It can be adapted to whatever degree of supervision you consider appropriate. Because the order of the chapters corresponds to the step-by-step process of preparing a paper, some classes can work independently. Because the chapters are organized in sections, they can also be covered by regular daily assignments. The goal throughout is to make the research procedure as simple and efficient as possible.

Each of the first five chapters is followed by exercises, some of which may be rather time-consuming. You may, therefore, choose to assign portions of an exercise either to individual students or to small groups. A sample paper is contained within the last chapter. The comments accompanying this paper (pp. 183–211) should be useful supplementary material because they are correlated with concrete instances in the paper.

Because notes and bibliographies are such unfamiliar territory for most students, there is a danger that they may be so intimidated by the intricacies of documentation that they neglect content and style. Thanks to publications of the Modern Language Association (*MLA Style Sheet*, 1951; rev. ed., 1970; and *MLA Handbook*, 1977), there is greater uniformity of documentation procedures in English than in most disciplines. Nevertheless, numerous variations exist to befuddle the beginning writer. Since the forms of notes and bibliographies are conventions rather than absolute rules, there will never be total uniformity. At present, new, simpler procedures are being widely adopted. This manual proposes sensible forms that can be adapted to the special problems that inevitably arise. Documentation is regarded as a convenience to the reader and not as a display of the writer's industry or ingenuity. In Chapter Five conventional forms are described and illustrated. Generally accepted variants are labeled in red type. If you have special preferences, ask students to star the variants you prefer. It would also be helpful to your students if you gave them answers to questions 15–20 in the Checklist (p. vii).

Various styles of documentation used in the Natural and Social Sciences are also described briefly and illustrated in Chapter Five (pp. 139–44). The most frequently used of these is that recommended by the American Psychological Association (APA style).

In 1982 an advisory committee of MLA proposed a drastically revised style of documentation, which brings practices in the Humanities closer to those in other disciplines. This style has been followed in *PMLA* since May, 1982. The new MLA style is described briefly in Chapter Five and is illustrated by a second version of the sample paper (pp. 214–26). Comparing the two versions of the same paper will demonstrate the basic features of the new system. You should determine which style will serve students best and which is more likely to be acceptable in their other courses.

The revised MLA forms simplify many cumbersome procedures, and students should understand them even though they follow conventional forms in their papers. Students will, of course, need to interpret conventional documentation in books and journals published before 1985. This manual, therefore, devotes considerable space to conventional forms for notes and bibliography, but the illustrative examples on pages 108–38 can readily be converted to the new MLA style.

A crucial question regarding a research paper is whether it should be considered as a finished product or as copy to be published. If considered as a finished product, it resembles published research as closely as possible. If considered as copy for publication, the notes, bibliography, and block quotations are double-spaced; Latin words and abbreviations are not underlined; and no words are broken at the end of a line. This procedure, which understandably is favored by MLA, is intended to facilitate the work of editors and typesetters. A sensible form for advanced graduate students to follow, it is not particularly useful to undergraduates, who are learning to interpret published research rather than to produce it. Both possibilities are discussed in Chapter Five, but a student's first research paper should probably be regarded as a finished product and should follow the conventions of published research.

The headnote quotations are taken from the writings of Samuel Johnson, whose example of diligence and downright common sense may sustain both you and your students throughout the tribulations and triumphs of research.

TO THE STUDENT

Your composition class and many of the courses you will take in other disciplines require that you write a relatively long essay based on facts and ideas collected from a variety of sources. Such an essay is variously known as a research paper, a library paper, a term paper, a source paper, or a documented paper. You will probably find more colorful terms for it.

Whatever the paper is called, it is not just an ordeal by footnote devised to occupy your time. In general, it requires that, on the basis of intensive reading, you reach some thoughtful conclusions, develop your ideas in an organized essay, and document your evidence. The ability to use a library and take notes efficiently, to analyze and interpret those notes, to organize your ideas and express them clearly, and to document borrowed facts and opinions will be extremely useful to you throughout your college career. Furthermore, the ability to gather, interpret, and organize information is a valuable skill in almost any business or profession. The purpose of this manual is to assist you in attaining and using this skill.

RESEARCH PAPERS
CHECKLIST

Do not imagine that you shall always remember even what perhaps you now think it impossible to forget.

Be certain that by the time your instructor has described the research paper assignment, you have clear-cut answers to the questions below. Some matters undoubtedly will be left to your discretion.

1. What are the minimum and maximum word limits?
2. Should the paper be a report or an evaluation? (See pp. 2–3.)
3. Are any kinds of sources (for example, encyclopedias and popular magazines) unacceptable?
4. Is advance approval of a topic required?
5. Is an outline to be included with the paper?
6. Is a topic outline, a sentence outline, or a combination outline preferred? (See pp. 86–90.)
7. Is a handwritten manuscript acceptable?
8. Is use of the first person acceptable?
9. Should the paper be fastened in a binder?
10. What information should appear on the title page?
11. Is a minimum number of sources required?
12. Are note cards to be handed in with the paper?
13. Is the rough draft to be handed in?
14. When is the completed paper due?

15. Are footnotes or endnotes preferred? (See p. 124.)
16. Should the publisher be included in a note?
17. Should Arabic or Roman numerals be used for volumes?
18. Should each note, bibliography entry, and block quotation be single-spaced or double-spaced?
19. Should Latin words and abbreviations be underlined?

20. Are the following procedures acceptable:

internal citation? (See pp. 136–37.)
split notes? (See pp. 137–38.)
shortened or abbreviated titles? (See p. 137.)
military style of writing dates? (See p. 110.)
postal abbreviations for states? (See p. 166.)
new MLA style of documentation? (See p. 145–61.)

RESEARCH PAPERS
TIMETABLE

Life, however short, is made still shorter by waste of time.

When your research paper is assigned, estimate the time that each phase will require. Set a date for the completion of each phase and record it in the first column. Later, record the date when each is completed.

	Date Due	*Date Done*
Topic narrowed	_____	_____
Preliminary bibliography compiled	_____	_____
Purposive reading begun	_____	_____
Thesis formulated	_____	_____
Main topics chosen	_____	_____
Working outline prepared	_____	_____
Note-taking completed	_____	_____
First draft written	_____	_____
Revision	_____	_____
Second draft written	_____	_____
Revision	_____	_____
Final copy written	_____	_____
Proofreading	_____	_____
Paper handed in	_____	_____

ONE
CHOOSING A TOPIC

Not even Shakespeare can write well without a proper subject.

The first step in the research process is choosing a suitable topic. In doing research, as the second syllable of the word implies, you look for information. Seeking material is only part of the task, however; you also analyze, interpret, organize, and write the results of your research.

THE RESEARCH PROCESS

Although you will use this manual to prepare a research paper for one class, it should acquaint you with a basic procedure applicable to many assignments, from brief reports to full-scale term papers. The research process involves the following steps:

1. Defining a problem
2. Collecting and evaluating material
3. Formulating a hypothesis
4. Organizing supporting material
5. Writing and documenting the results

You may wish that research, like measles or a fraternity initiation, was something to undergo only once, but it actually involves a process that you will follow many times in other courses and in later life. The basic research process with some modifications is followed by a lawyer searching casebooks for precedents, a politician studying public opinion polls, a reporter investigating a tax scandal, a football coach scouting his next opponent, a prospective car-buyer comparing the new models, or a garden club member preparing a talk on tuberous begonias.

Though termed a "process," preparation of a research paper is not a recipe to be followed step by step or a mechanical, assembly line operation. As in most endeavors, false starts, duplication of effort, time-wasting, and outright blunders are inevitable. To minimize such frustrations, this manual points out possible pitfalls and traces the procedure from the choice of a topic to the final proofreading. Still, no two people work in just the same way, and you should adapt the suggested procedures to your own work habits. You will often be engaged in two or more phases of the process simultaneously. At times you will need to turn back to a phase already discussed, and at other times you will need to look ahead to phases not yet covered in class. Before starting your research, read the sample paper and commentary (pp. 183–211) for a general impression of form and content in a typical research paper.

A WORK SCHEDULE

A research paper is always assigned several weeks in advance, and you should start working on it as soon as possible. If your instructor suggests dates when the various phases should be completed, try to stay ahead of that schedule or, at least, keep up with it. Otherwise, draw up your own schedule and follow it. The Timetable on page ix is a convenient place to record your commitments and log your progress.

Many students have a superstitious faith in the value of desperate all-night sessions to meet an assignment. You probably could spend two days in the library and two nights at your typewriter and produce a paper, but the results would almost certainly be eyestrain, frazzled nerves, and a mediocre paper. A successful research paper is not written in a frenzied burst of energy but evolves slowly through continued effort. Collecting and organizing material will take more time than you expect. Despite temptations to postpone work, start looking for a topic and collecting material as soon as the paper is assigned.

KINDS OF PAPERS

Be sure that you understand whether your instructor expects a **report** or an **evaluation.** The first is a record of your research; the second is a product of it.

Report

A chronological account of Custer's defeat at Little Big Horn, for example, would be a report. A report requires skill in choosing sources, in abstracting material from them, and in documenting borrowed facts and opinions. Its chief purpose is to report (literally, to carry back) the results of your reading. A report may be based on a single source.

Evaluation

A report is concerned chiefly with **who** or **what,** but an evaluation considers **why** or **how.** A report develops a topic. An evaluation develops both a topic and a **thesis**—a purpose, an interpretive judgment, a central idea that will unify your paper. An evaluation not only presents information but also analyzes it. For example, an attempt to show why Custer was defeated or why his Last Stand is so widely known would be an evaluation. To write an evaluation, you acquaint yourself thoroughly with a narrow topic, reach certain conclusions, and support those conclusions with material from various authorities. A valid thesis is essential. An evaluation requires originality and imagination and always draws on a variety of sources.

UNSUITABLE TOPICS

If your instructor assigns a topic, your first task is to find a workable thesis. If your class is using a controlled-research casebook or if a broad subject like Popular Culture or Space Exploration is assigned to the entire class, you will need to find a narrow topic and a workable thesis. If you have a free choice, you need to explore a general subject that interests you to find a narrow topic and a workable thesis. In general, if a topic can be described by any of the five terms below, it is unsuitable or, at best, involves special hazards.

1. **Too broad.** Because a research paper is relatively long, there is a natural temptation to choose a broad subject. But if the assignment is 2,000 words, the paper will be about eight or nine typed pages, about the length of a full column and a half in a newspaper. It is impossible to cover "The American Indian" or "The History of Sculpture" in that much space. Biographical papers are often unsuccessful because they attempt to cover the subject's entire life, and they often lack a meaningful thesis. If you write about an individual, focus on one aspect of that person's career.
2. **Too subjective.** A personal notion or attitude that cannot readily be supported by facts and opinions from printed sources would be a poor topic. It would be difficult to find support in the library for "Why I Joined a Fraternity" or "Blondes Have More Fun."
3. **Too controversial.** A highly controversial topic may be risky for two reasons: the ambiguous nature of the material and your own preconceptions or prejudices. With some subjects reliable information may be unavailable, or contradictory charges and countercharges may defy your efforts to sift the true from the false. Watergate, Three Mile Island, and the Right to Life movement, for example, are probably too complex for limited research. You may feel so

strongly about a controversial subject that you cannot weigh the evidence objectively.

4. **Too familiar.** A research paper should take you into new territory. Work in the library should produce a thrill of discovery, not bored recognition of the already-known. If, for example, you are an expert on airmail stamps, material that you collect on that subject would already be familiar, and the job would soon become tedious. Do not write on a topic you have already investigated for another course, and, above all, do not hand in a paper previously written for another course. The first is foolish because retracing familiar ground soon becomes monotonous; the second is dishonest, will be considered plagiarism, and will probably result in a failing grade.

5. **Too technical.** The decision as to whether a topic is too technical for you to investigate will depend on your background and interests. A paper on "Use of Radioactive Tracers in Plant Culture" would be suitable for a student with some prior knowledge of the field but not for a student wholly untrained in science. In general, do not pick a subject involving totally unfamiliar concepts and terms.

EXPLORATORY READING

After a research paper is first assigned, you will probably think first of a broad subject like pollution, politics, or photography. Each of these is obviously too broad for an essay, or even for a book. The purpose of exploratory reading is to discover a narrow topic and a sound, workable thesis.

Encyclopedias, handbooks, and general magazines are best for this type of reading. Your goal is wide coverage of a subject to discover some narrow topic that interests you. While you are browsing through a general source, for example, the author's casual reference to a minor point may arouse your curiosity and start you on a search of more specialized sources. Your paper should not duplicate work done in another course, but it may derive from it. A remark in your American History class about the Zouaves, colorful Northern troops in the Civil War, might send you to the library to look for more information.

Taking notes while exploring a subject is a waste of time. Read rapidly but alertly. Postpone note-taking until you are firmly committed to a topic and a thesis.

A TENTATIVE PLAN
(Exercise A)

Narrowing a Topic

There is no more fatal error than trying to write on a comprehensive subject that could scarcely be covered in a book. Broad subjects like the women's liberation movement, dogs, or American history must be pared down considerably. You will probably need to narrow a subject several times before reducing it to a workable topic. For example:

American history
The West
Indians
The Sioux
Tribal organization
Sioux uprisings after the Civil War
Custer's Last Stand

Some of this narrowing will be effortless. No one would seriously consider writing a research paper on any of the first four subjects above. The later stages become more difficult. You may resist the necessity of limiting a subject because it seems easier to find material on a broad subject. However, the more limited your topic, the more specific you can be in developing it. Trim a subject down; shrink it until it fits the assignment.

Formulating a Thesis

Reducing a subject in scope is only half your task. If you narrow the women's liberation movement to the Equal Rights Amendment, dogs to Chihuahuas, or American history to Custer's Last Stand, you still have no basis for deciding what material to include and what to exclude. If your paper is to be an evaluation, you need a thesis.

An **effective thesis** is not discovered in your reading; it is formulated while you read or while you think about what you have read. It should be the product of your own thinking, not an idea that you find ready-made in a book. The thesis is a one-sentence statement of your topic and your central idea, your approach to the topic. It controls what sort of material you will look for. The best method of discovering a thesis is to ask yourself questions while doing the exploratory reading: *Why were the Sioux mobilized? What was their strategy? Why was Custer defeated? Why is the Custer legend so well known?* In its final form, however, the thesis should be a declarative statement. It is often derived from a cause–effect relationship: *The Custer legend is well known because . . . .* The student who narrowed American history to Custer's Last Stand might start with the following statement: *The story of Custer's Last Stand is one of the most interesting episodes in Western history.* The inadequacy of this thesis would soon become apparent. The word "interesting" (popular as a perfunctory choice of students formulating a thesis) is so broad that it would admit almost any material into the paper. Dissatisfaction with a preliminary thesis may lead to further narrowing of the topic.

The student might focus on the aftermath of Custer's battle, the legend that most Americans know. The narrowed topic would produce a revised thesis: *Custer's Last Stand is a legend with which almost every American is familiar.* This statement is a considerable improvement, and the student could safely begin taking notes. It is somewhat misleading, however, because it does not clearly indicate that the paper will analyze reasons for the familiarity. Recognition that various incidental aspects of the event made it legendary might produce this statement: *Various aspects of Custer's Last Stand that appeal to the imagination and the emotions have made it one of the best known events in American history.* This thesis would be acceptable and would serve as a guide in choosing and organizing material.

Ordinarily the thesis is the most difficult sentence in the entire paper to write. You may try several versions before you arrive at a satisfactory statement. Keep revising until the sentence clearly expresses your topic and its significance. Avoid vague or ambiguous terms like "interesting." If, after conscientious effort, you are absolutely unable to compose a satisfactory thesis sentence, you probably should choose a different topic.

Selecting Main Topics

When you begin reading purposefully, use one note card to list possible points that might be developed in the paper. Such topics often result from free association as one idea suggests another. The following items may have occurred to the student writing about Custer:

1. Custer's troops
2. The Sioux
3. Paintings of the battle
4. The fight
5. The terrain
6. Reasons for the legend being so well known
7. Custer's previous career
8. Arguments about the battle
9. Stories of survivors
10. Background of the battle
11. Movie versions
12. Newspaper accounts
13. Custer's responsibility for the defeat
14. Later record of the Seventh Cavalry
15. Mrs. Custer

In considering this list, the student may have reasoned somewhat as follows: Topics 1, 2, 4, 5, 10, and 13 pertain to the battle. It must be described but as briefly as posible. Therefore, 1, 2, 5, and 13 are not worth extended treatment. This leaves 4 and 10:

The fight
Background of the battle

The order, of course, would be reversed in the paper.

Of the remaining topics, 6 is almost as broad as the thesis and should be cut. Topic 7 seems dubious, but it suggests that Custer's celebrity resulting from earlier military exploits contributed to the legend. Topic 8 also seems questionable, but if controversy kept the legend alive it can be retained. Topic 11 is promising, although the student might have to use histories of film for accounts of movie versions. Topics 3, 9, and 12 pertain to the legend; topics 14 and 15 do not. This leaves 3, 7, 8, 9, and 12:

Paintings of the battle
Custer's previous career
Arguments about the battle
Stories of survivors
Newspaper accounts

Some may be combined, and some may be eliminated altogether. The most suitable order would be determined later.

Having settled on a narrow topic, a thesis, and seven tentative main points, the student would be ready to begin collecting titles of possible sources and taking notes.

When you reach this stage in preparing your own paper, request a brief conference with your instructor. Ask for guidance in evaluating your thesis, structuring the topics, and locating sources.

PRELIMINARY BIBLIOGRAPHY - *List of sources*
(Exercise B)

When you have chosen a narrow topic, composed a tentative thesis, and considered possible divisions of your topic, you should begin compiling a **bibliography**—a card file of useful-looking sources. For this purpose 3 × 5 cards are most efficient. Write only one source on a card so that cards listing unproductive sources can be set aside and the remainder can be alphabetized easily. If a source contains nothing useful, write "No help," "Zilch," or some other code term on the card so that you do not waste time by returning to that source later.

Include on each card the information that belongs in a bibliography (see p. 108). Punctuating the card like a formal bibliographical entry reduces the possibility of later transcription errors. Listing the call number of a book or the location of a journal and a brief note on the content or the way you expect to use it will also be helpful. These notes are for your own guidance, of course, and do not appear in the final bibliography. Be sure to include all bibliographical information even though you are not absolutely sure that you will use the source. It is depressing, to say the least, to discover while typing the final draft of a paper that a publisher's name or the title of an article is missing. Such discoveries usually occur late at night when the library is closed.

The titles of sources for the preliminary bibliography are gleaned from the library card catalog, from periodical indexes, and from printed bibliographies. If you are doubtful about whether a book will be useful, find a copy in the stacks and scan the index. If your topic is not listed, you are unlikely to use the book, and writing a bibliography card would be a waste of time. In collecting titles of magazine articles, make out cards only for magazines available in your library unless you

Fenin, George N., and William K.
Everson. *The Western from
Silents to the Seventies.*

New York: Grossman, 1973.

PN
1795
.9   (*Little Big Man*, p. 370)
W4
F45

Sample bibliography card for a book

Holbrook, Stewart H. "Phonies of
the Old West." *American
Mercury,* Feb. 1949,
pp. 230-35.

(good survivor story)

Sample bibliography card for a magazine article

plan to visit other libraries. The periodicals in your library will be listed in a vertical file, on a computer print-out, or on microforms. Ask a librarian for assistance.

Compiling a preliminary bibliography is a test of your topic. As you collect sources, you may discover less material than you expected. You must, therefore, either expand the topic or abandon it. Students frequently complain that there is not enough material in the library. Usually such complaints are not justified. They often mean that there are not a dozen books with the same title as the student's essay. Books and magazine articles on related subjects would probably furnish enough material. The "nothing in the library" excuse is certainly overworked. No library is complete, of course, but your library contains information on most of the subjects you are likely to investigate. However, if you cannot find the material, the result is the same as though it were not there. The sooner you discover a shortage of material and revise your topic, the better. More often, the compilation of a preliminary bibliography results in an embarrassment of riches; there is so much material that the topic must be narrowed.

Exploratory reading, narrowing a topic, analyzing it in relation to a viable thesis and possible main divisions, and compiling a card file of sources are not wholly separate procedures to be completed in sequence. Most or all of them are underway simultaneously during the early stages of your research.

Exercise A   Devising a Tentative Plan

Begin with a general subject-field that you are considering for your research paper and reduce it in scope at least five times as American history was reduced to Custer's Last Stand (p. 5). The final item should be the most specific in the sequence.

Subject _____

1. _____
2. _____
3. _____
4. _____
5. _____

Tentative Topic _____

Sometimes a title is a useful means of narrowing a topic. Devise a possible title for the topic above.

Title _____

Let your mind "free-associate" over the title you have chosen. List at least eight related aspects or phases of it that occur to you.

1. _____
2. _____
3. _____
4. _____
5. _____
6. _____
7. _____
8. _____

Compose a thesis sentence that would cover at least five of the topics above. Remember that it would undoubtedly be modified on the basis of your research.

Tentative Thesis _____

_____

_____

Exercise B   Preparing a Preliminary Bibliography

Using the information provided, make a bibliography card for each of the following sources. (See pp. 7–8.)

A book by David Minter entitled William Faulkner: His Life and Work and published by Johns Hopkins University Press in Baltimore in 1980.

A book edited by Joseph Blotner entitled Selected Letters of William Faulkner and published by Random House of New York City in 1977.

An article by Harold Hungerford entitled Past and Present in Light in August published in volume 55 of American Literature in the issue of May, 1983, on pages 183–98.

TWO
USING THE LIBRARY

When we enquire into any subject, the first thing we have to do is to know what books have treated of it. This leads us to look at catalogues and at the backs of books in libraries.

Despite the attractions of the student union, the gymnasium, or the laboratory, the library is the most important building on your college campus. Perhaps you have already discovered its value as a meeting place and, more importantly, as a quiet spot for day-to-day studying with reference books conveniently at hand, as a collection of books and magazines for leisure reading, and as a source of reference materials for reports and term papers. To prepare a satisfactory research paper, you must be able to use library resources efficiently. Your first research paper will inevitably involve false starts and wasted effort, but as you become familiar with the card catalog, the periodical indexes, and other tools of research, you will develop a research strategy that will make future papers easier to write.

LIBRARY FLOOR PLAN
(Exercises C and D)

Libraries differ in various ways, of course, but basic procedures are similar enough that if you become familiar with your college library, you can quickly adapt to any other that you may visit. Perhaps, as a new student, you have been taken on an orientation tour. You should follow this with your own exploration. An excellent way to familiarize yourself with the library is to draw a simple floor plan. The main features will include the following:

1. **Main desk.** The main desk is the nerve center of the library. Here call slips are presented and books are charged out or returned. Librarians stationed here will answer your questions. Look for a source on your own before asking for help. Although they are subjected to many vague questions and unreasonable requests, librarians are incredibly accommodating. But do not begin your investigation of a subject by asking a librarian where the books are. Until you have looked for yourself, the librarian will direct you to the card catalog. When you have attempted to find material without success, then ask for assistance.

2. **Card catalog.** An alphabetical index of all books in the library, the card catalog is the most important tool in most research.

3. **Stacks.** The shelved books sometimes are not open to undergraduates. Even if you have access to the stacks, a search of the shelves may be misleading because important books are likely to be on loan, in special collections, or on the reserve shelves.

4. **Reference room.** Reference books are collections of information that are consulted rather than read consecutively. They are usually on open shelves in a special room and cannot be checked out. A reference librarian can direct you to sources of information if your request is clear and specific. General reference works such as encyclopedias are more or less useful in all fields; specialized works of various kinds are available in every field. Get to know the basic general works as well as the specialized ones in your major field of interest.

5. **Reserve section.** Books to be used in the library or withdrawn only for brief periods are placed on reserve. The most recent and most useful books in academic fields are often found here. A notation on the catalog card may indicate that a book has been placed on reserve, and a separate file listing reserve books is usually available.

6. **Periodicals section.** Current periodicals are usually arranged alphabetically in a reading room or some other central location. After they have been bound, the volumes are assigned call numbers and shelved according to their subject matter. If they have been replaced by microforms, that fact will be noted in the library's listing of its periodical holdings and in the card catalog.

7. **Readers and computer terminals.** Readers for microfilm and microforms are usually available in a special room. Large libraries are also rapidly expanding computer services with access to public and commercial data banks. To use these facilities for the first time, you are almost certain to need assistance from a librarian.

SOME USEFUL TERMS

Like all professionals, librarians have their own technical vocabulary. Some of the more common terms are defined below.

abstract A summary of the substance of a work. In some scholarly journals, an abstract precedes each article. Collections (for example, *Chemical Abstracts*) enable you to estimate the potential usefulness of articles before reading the originals.

analytical entry A catalog card for a portion of a book (for example, a play in an anthology).

annotated bibliography Identification and brief evaluation of each entry. Also called a critical bibliography.

cumulation The recombinaton of entries from several issues of a serial into a single alphabetized arrangement. (See the description of *Readers' Guide,* p. 25.)

data bank (also data base) A collection of computerized data (often bibliographical) available to subscribers to a public or a commercial computer service.

descriptor A reference to an entry in an index; for example, subject headings in a card catalog or key words in *Roget's Thesaurus.* The use of descriptors is increasing rapidly because they are well adapted to the retrieval of computerized data.

dictionary catalog A card catalog in which author, title, and subject cards are arranged in a single alphabetization.

divided catalog A card catalog in which author, title, and subject cards are filed in separate alphabetizations.

edition The bound copies of a book printed from a single setting of type. A new edition is presumably a revision.

entry A rather broad term for a unit of information recorded in a catalog, index, bibliography, or other listing.

journal Used in two senses: (1) a publication like a newspaper or weekly magazine dealing with current events; (2) a periodical intended for specialists, often termed a "scholarly journal" (for example, *Journal of Literary Semantics*).

online A computer term (generally written as one word) indicating that information is accessible.

periodical A publication that appears at regular intervals of more than one day.

quarterly A scholarly journal published four times a year (for example, *Southern Folklore Quarterly*).

review A periodical devoted chiefly to criticism (for example, *Sewanee Review*).

see also A cross-reference to another entry; used in catalogs and indexes like *Readers' Guide.* Sometimes abbreviated *sa.*

serial Any publication issued in a consecutive, indefinitely continuing series; for example, periodicals, newspapers, yearbooks, installments of a long work published in successive issues of a magazine.

shelf list A library's holdings arranged by call numbers, often in the form of a computer printout.

tracing (also called added entries) Descriptors on an entry in a catalog that indicate other headings under which a work is listed.

union catalog A card catalog of the holdings of a group of cooperating libraries. Useful for publication data as well as for the location of books not in your own library.

The following time-saving abbreviations are in widespread use:

BIP *Books in Print.* Annual author, title, and subject indexes of books currently available from publishers.

CBEL *Cambridge Bibliography of English Literature.* The revised edition is designated *NCBEL.*

CBI *Cumulative Book Index.* A monthly author, title, and subject listing of books published in English. Annual and biennial cumulations.

CIS Congressional Information Service (publisher of indexes to government publications).

DAB *Dictionary of American Biography.*

DAE *Dictionary of American English.*

DNB *Dictionary of National Biography* (British).

ERIC Educational Resources Information Center. (See pp. 25, 27.)

f Folio, a book more than fifteen inches high. On a catalog entry, "f" indicates that a book is large and is not shelved in accordance with its call number. Ask a librarian where oversized books are located.

GPO Government Printing Office.

LC Library of Congress.

LHUS *Literary History of the United States.*

NCBEL *New Cambridge Bibliography of English Literature.*

NED *New English Dictionary.* Original title of *OED.*

OED *Oxford English Dictionary.*

Per Periodical. In a catalog entry, indicates that a work is shelved in the Periodical Room.

q Quarto, a book eleven to fifteen inches high. (See "f" above.)

Ref Reference. In a catalog entry, indicates that a work is shelved in the Reference Room.

TLS (London) *Times Literary Supplement.*

ULS *Union List of Serials.* A listing of American magazines, their publishing history, and libraries where they can be found.

CATALOGS
(Exercise E)

A **card catalog** or a **computerized catalog** is a bibliography of all the books in a library. It may also include entries for other materials such as cassettes, films, microforms, and periodicals. As such, it is the starting point for most library research.

Using the Card Catalog

A card catalog is designed to enable you to locate a book even though you have only partial information. In gathering material for a paper on the Santa Fe Trail, you may recall the name of Josiah Gregg from class discussion. Under "Gregg" you will find an author card for his book *Commerce of the Prairies.* Perhaps, on the other hand, you recall only the title of the book; a title card will be found under "Commerce." Perhaps you know neither author nor title. By looking under general subject headings like "Santa Fe Trail," "Southwest," and "Mexico," you can locate Gregg's book and others on the same subject.

A useful source during the early stages of research is *Subject Headings,* two large volumes published by the Library of Congress. It lists alphabetically all of the subject headings or descriptors under which cards are filed. It is usually located near the card catalog and can be examined much more easily than a dozen separate file drawers. If, for example, you were considering a paper on some aspect of modern painting and turned to "Modern Art," you would be referred to "Art, Modern—20th Century." Under that caption you would find references to several schools of painting, beginning with "Cubism" and closing with "Surrealism." By looking at cards under one or more of these headings, you would find relevant title cards.

A book is ordinarily listed at least three times—on an author card, on a title card, and on at least one subject card. Frequently, it will have several subject listings. It may also be listed under the name of a joint author, an editor, an illustrator, or a translator.

A card catalog in a large library may contain several million entries. Author, title, and subject entries are usually filed in one alphabetical sequence—a **dictionary catalog.** However, some libraries maintain an author catalog, a title catalog, and a subject catalog—**a divided catalog.** Such an enormous collection of information obviously requires uniform procedures in arranging and alphabetizing the cards. Some library practices useful to remember are the following:

1. Works by a person are listed first; works about that person follow. This sequence is very significant in a large library. In the Library of Congress, for example, the Shakespeare cards take up seventeen file drawers.
2. Abbreviations and numerals are alphabetized as though spelled out in full. *2001: A Space Odyssey* will be filed under "T."
3. Names beginning with Mc and M' are filed as though spelled Mac.
4. In titles, prefixes like *de* or *von* and articles (*a, an, the,* and articles in foreign languages) are disregarded. In author's names, however, some libraries con-

sider prefixes as part of the word. For example, cards for the poet Walter De la Mare may be filed as though the surname were spelled Delamare.

5. Most libraries follow the practice of alphabetizing word-by-word rather than letter-by-letter. New York will be filed before Newfoundland and Fort Moultrie before Fortification.

6. If the same word is used for a person, a place, and a title, the cards are filed in that order. For example:

> Washington, George
> Washington, D.C.
> *Washington Square* (a novel)

Many minor variations in procedures are possible and can best be clarified by your asking a librarian for assistance.

The author entry is the basic form or "main entry." To make title and subject cards, library catalogers type a book's title or its subject above the author's name. All other information is the same. The sample author card below illustrates the information found in a card catalog. Most of the facts below the fourth line are technical data for librarians. Notice, however, the tracing; the subject headings and other entries under which cards for a book are filed may be useful to you.

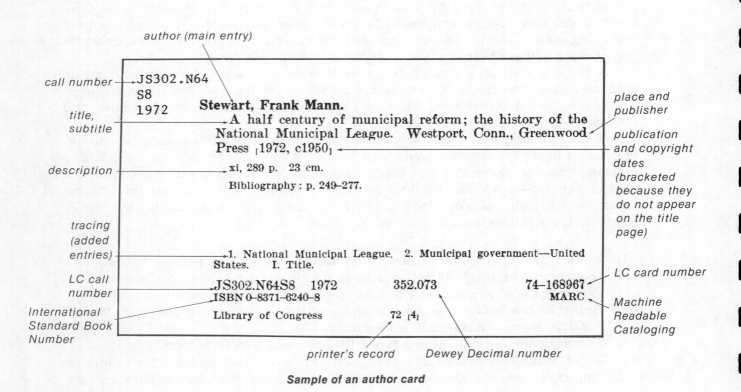

Sample of an author card

Most cards in your school library catalog will resemble the example above. New cards, however, repeat the author's name after the title and use somewhat different punctuation. The basic information is the same. The purpose of the revised form is to facilitate computerization.

Robbins, Peter.
  Guide to non-ferrous metals and their markets / Peter Robbins. — 3rd ed. — New York : Nichols Pub. Co., 1982.
  183 p. : ill. ; 24 cm.
  Rev. ed. of: Guide to non-ferrous metals and their markets / John Edwards and Peter Robbins. 1979.
  ISBN 0-89397-124-3 : $45.00

  1. Nonferrous metal industries.   2. Market surveys.   I. Edwards, John. Guide to non-ferrous metals and their markets.   II. Title.
  HD9539.A2R63   1982   380.1'45669—dc19   81-18897
                                                            AACR 2   MARC
  Library of Congress

Sample of a new-style author card

Using a Computerized Catalog

Your school library will probably make a drastic revision of its cataloging procedures soon, if it has not already done so. Most large libraries have begun or are considering a shift to a catalog based on computerized information (often nicknamed "Comcat"). The Library of Congress, which sets the pace for American libraries, has added no new cards to its catalog since 1980. Essentially the new system involves local, regional, and national data banks, where information regarding books is stored on computer tape. Using a terminal with access to the data bank, you can punch out a symbol for the author, title, or subject of a book and receive the information now printed on a catalog card.

A library can also have all the data now in its card catalog recorded on a computer printout or, more probably, on microfiche or some other type of microform. The major advantages of the new system are economy and accessibility. It saves the space now taken up by card catalogs and the expense of purchasing and filing cards. Because microfiche is relatively inexpensive, readers and sets of fiche can be made available at various locations in the library and even in departmental offices and dormitories. The conventions that control the arrangement of information and the method of classifying books will remain the same. Computerized cataloging is, therefore, a change in the form but not in the content or purpose of a card catalog.

Locating Sources

Four practical suggestions may save you some time and annoyance:

1. Be alert for sources indirectly related to your topic. When you are investigating a topic, its importance becomes distorted. You feel that any book pertaining to your subject should be listed in the catalog under that heading. Sometimes a useful discussion of your topic will be found on a single page of a book on a different, although related, subject. Use *Subject Headings,* "see also" entries in the catalog, and your imagination to discover relevant sources. If you were writing a paper on poltergeists, you might find no title cards under that heading but cross-references to "Apparitions" and "Demonology." Consulting *Subject Headings* and using your ingenuity, you would also look in the catalog under "Ghosts," "Spirits," "Invisible World," and "Psychical Research."
2. When you find a title, copy its call number accurately. Omitting one letter or numeral may make it impossible to find the book.
3. When you find a book in the stacks, look at the books on either side of it. They will be related in subject matter, even though you did not discover them while searching the catalog.
4. If your book is not on the shelf, it probably has been checked out, but it may have been misshelved. Look at the shelves above and below, and look behind the books to be sure that it has not been accidentally pushed out of sight. Occasionally the book you need will be found on the cart holding books to be reshelved.

Classification of Books

In a large library, which may contain a million or more volumes, some foolproof system for locating each book is necessary. For this reason, each book is assigned a specific code symbol or call number; this symbol, consisting of numbers and letters, is found on the spine of a book and on all catalog entries for that book.

The first line of a call number is the classification number, which will be uniform in all libraries using the same system. The lower line or lines are the author number, a combination of the initial letter of an author's last name, code numbers, and sometimes the first letter of the title. The author number identifies the precise location of a book. For example, if a library using the Library of Congress system has books on the Battle of Gettysburg by Clifford Dowdey, Earl S. Miers, and Glenn Tucker, each will have the same classification number (E 474.51). The author numbers will differ, however, and the books will be shelved as follows:

D74   (Dowdey)
M5   (Miers)
T83   (Tucker)

The two classification systems in common use are the **Dewey Decimal** and the **Library of Congress.** You should know the general nature of the system used in your library, as well as the categories that apply to your major field of study.

1. **The Dewey Decimal system,** as the name suggests, is based on numerals divisible by ten. The fields of knowledge are divided into ten general categories:

000–099	General Works	500–599	Pure Science
100–199	Philosophy	600–699	Applied Arts and Sciences
200–299	Religion	700–799	Fine Arts, Recreation
300–399	Social Sciences	800–899	Literature
400–499	Philology	900–999	History, Geography, Travel, Biography

   Each general category is subdivided by tens. For example:

500–509	Pure Science	550–559	Geology
510–519	Mathematics	560–569	Paleontology
520–529	Astronomy	570–579	Biology
530–539	Physics	580–589	Botany
540–549	Chemistry	590–599	Zoology

   Each of these fields is also subdivided. For example:

510	Mathematics	515	Descriptive geometry
511	Arithmetic	516	Analytic geometry
512	Algebra	517	Calculus
513	Geometry	518	Unassigned
514	Trigonometry	519	Probabilities

   Each specific category is subdivided further by adding numbers after the decimal. For example:

511	Arithmetic	511.5	Analysis
511.1	Systems	511.6	Proportion
511.2	Numeration	511.7	Involution, evolution
511.3	Prime numbers	511.8	Mercantile rules
511.4	Fractions	511.9	Problems and tables

   A weakness of the Dewey Decimal system is that since it was devised in the 1870's, the vast expansion of knowledge in Social Sciences (the 300's) and Pure Science (the 500's) has made these categories inadequate. Classification numbers are often long and cumbersome.

2. **The Library of Congress system,** which is based on letters, is preferred by most large libraries. Because there are twenty-one main categories instead of only ten, classification requires fewer symbols. The major categories are as follows:

A   General works, Polygraphy
B   Philosophy, Religion
C   History, Auxiliary sciences
D   History, Topography (except America)
E   America (general), United States (general)
F   United States (local), America (except the United States)
G   Geography, Anthropology
H   Social Sciences (general), Statistics, Economics, Sociology
J   Political Science
K   Law
L   Education
M   Music
N   Fine Arts
P   Language and Literature
Q   Science
R   Medicine
S   Agriculture
T   Technology
U   Military Science
V   Naval Science
Z   Bibliography, Library Science

Further subdivision is accomplished by an added letter and, when necessary, one or more numbers. Below are the principal subdivisions of "S," one of the simplest categories:

S   General agriculture, soils, fertilizers, implements
SB   General plant culture, horticulture, parks, pests
SD   Forestry
SF   Animal culture, veterinary medicine
SH   Fish culture, fisheries
SK   Hunting, game protection

INDEXES

Readers' Guide
(Exercise E)

Next to the card catalog, the most useful research tool in a library is *Readers' Guide to Periodical Literature,* an index to more than a hundred general magazines. When you become familiar with its system of arrangement, you will also be able to use numerous specialized indexes that are similarly arranged. Since it would be impossible for anyone to examine issues of a hundred magazines even for one month, indexes like *Readers' Guide* are indispensable.

Readers' Guide is published twice a month except in July and August, when it appears monthly. The second issue each month cumulates the first in one alphabetical arrangement. Similarly, three-, six-, and nine-month cumulations include all information in that year's previous issues. At the end of each year, a bound volume replaces the soft-cover cumulations. Two-year cumulations are published in odd-numbered years. Early volumes of *Readers' Guide* covered four years; since 1935, however, each permanent volume has covered two years.

In an enormous index like this, space must be conserved whenever possible. The system of abbreviations and other shortcuts may bewilder you at first, so that you will need to consult the key at the beginning of the volume. Author and subject entries resemble those in a card catalog: an article is listed under the author's name and under at least one subject heading. Titles of articles are seldom main entries, but short stories and plays are listed by title.

Some conventions used in *Readers' Guide* are illustrated in the facsimile on page 26.

ERIC

A comprehensive index to less accessible materials is provided by Educational Research Information Center (ERIC). Many students overlook this reference work because it is relatively new and because they assume that it is designed only for courses in Education.

If you begin with a general subject in mind, your first step is to look in the most recent edition of *Thesaurus of ERIC Descriptors.* Similar to *Subject Headings,* this volume lists terms or general topics and related terms or subtopics under which material is indexed. Under FEMINISM, for example, you would find six subtopics: CIVIL RIGHTS, FEMALES, LIFE STYLE, SEX DISCRIMINATION, SEX FAIRNESS, and WOMEN'S STUDIES. Your next step would be to consult a semiannual volume of *Resources in Education,* an index to papers, reports, and other documents, many of which have not been formally published. Under SEX DISCRIMINATION, you would find nineteen entries, including the title of a paper: "When Is Unequal Unfair: The Role of Ideology." It would be identified by an "educational document" number: ED 218 530.

By looking at the spines of the monthly issues of *Resources in Education,* you would find that the December, 1982, issue contains educational documents 218 416 through 219 495. By looking under 218 530, you would find that it designates a paper by Janet Weinglass and Janice M. Steil, the paper is 28 pages long, and it was presented at the American Psychological Association convention in Los Angeles in August of 1981. Finally, and most importantly, you would find an abstract of the paper, which would enable you to judge its relevance to your subject. It is important to remember that abstracts appear in the monthly issues but not in the semiannual indexes. However, annual collections of abstracts, which are identified by the same ED numbers as in the monthly indexes, are published separately.

If your library subscribes to the complete ERIC service, you could find the paper reproduced on microfiche and indexed under ED 218 530. If your library does not have microfiche, another library in your area may be a subscriber. If all else fails, you can purchase copies of many papers from ERIC Document Reproduction Service, PO Box 190, Arlington, Va., 22210.

Sea trout fishing *See* Weakfish fishing ← cross-reference from one viable
Sea urchins heading to another
 See also
  Cooking—Shellfish
Sea water
 Abyssal water carbon-14 distribution and the age of the
  world oceans. M. Stuiver and others. bibl f il *Science*
  219:849-51 F 18 '83
 Biological control of the removal of abiogenic particles   ← articles with
  from the surface ocean [aluminum in the Sargasso   bibliography,
  Sea] W. G. Deuser and others. bibl f il *Science*   footnotes,
  219:388-91 Ja 28 '83   illustrations
 Why is the sea salty? il *Sci Dig* 91:91 F '83
     Desalting
   See Saline water conversion ← subdivisions of topic
     Pollution
   See Marine pollution
Seabed mining *See* Ocean mining
Seabirds *See* Sea birds
Seafaring life ← cross-references
 See also
  Voyages
Seafirst Corporation   magazine with no
 Cooley's interstate strategy for Seafirst. *Bus Week* p81←   volume number
  Ja 10 '83
 Seattle rescue. il *Time* 121:54 Ja 31 '83
Seafood
 See also
  Cooking—Seafood
  Fish as food ← cross-references
Seafood, Frozen
 See also
  Fish, Frozen
Seafood contamination *See* Fish contamination
Seafood gathering
 See also   type of article
  Shellfish gathering

subject → **Seaga, Edward P. G.**
     about
 We have had our recession [interview] A. D. Frank.   magazine volume:
  por *Forbes* 131:44+ Ja 3 '83 ←   pages, issue

author → **Seal, David**
 Astronomy in Egypt: a monument for Alexandria. il
title of article →   *Sky Telesc* 65:168-70 F '83
Sealing
 EEC harp-seal ban may save some pups. J. Raloff. *Sci*
  News 123:150 Mr 5 '83
title of article . author → One last fling on the floes? [ban on imports of Canadian
  seal pelts by European Community] R. Joyce and M.
  Goldstick. il *Macleans* 96:15 Mr 14 '83
Sealing compounds
 See also
  Caulking
Seals (Animals)
  See also
  Sealing
 Demography of northern elephant seals, 1911-1982. C.
  F. Cooper and B. S. Stewart. bibl f il *Science* 219:969-71
  F 25 '83
 Elephant seals rise from near extinction. il *Sci News*
  123:134 F 26 '83
map → Holy mackerel! Moritz the sea elephant really knows
  how to sing for his supper. il *People Wkly* 19:101
  F 7 '83
 Hoover [talking harbor seal] *New Yorker* 58:25-7 Ja 3
  '83
 When summer comes to the Aucklands. F. Bruemmer.
  il map *Int Wildl* 13:41-7 Mr/Ap '83 ← bimonthly magazine
Search for Extraterrestrial Intelligence *See* Interstellar
 communication   portrait
Search Ministries
 Putting lifestyle evangelism to work. L. Moody. por *Christ*
  Today 27:14 Ja 7 '83
subject → **Searches and seizures**   brief indication of
 A case of anonymity [case of E. Lawson] J. Nelson.   content
  por *Black Enterp* 13:26 Mr '83
 Good intentions, bad results [exclusionary rule] M. S.
  Forbes, Jr. il *Forbes* 131:23 F 28 '83
 Is the ACLU being reasonable? [stand against vehicle
  checks in drunken driving cases] G. F. Will. il *Newsweek*
  101:80 Ja 31 '83

Facsimile page from Readers' Guide to Periodical Literature

Citation Indexes

Somewhat similar indexing methods and more comprehensive coverage are found in three computer-produced reference works covering periodicals and some books: *Science Citation Index, Social Sciences Citation Index,* and *Arts & Humanities Citation Index.* They differ in minor ways, but the basic format is the same. If you learn to use one of them, you will be able to use the other two. Because they index articles by three different methods, the same article may be listed a dozen or more times. They are designed to enable you to find a source even though you have only partial information. You can "enter" (begin using) the indexes with any of the volumes described below.

1. *Permuterm Subject Index.* A permuterm is a descriptor, a key term taken from the title of an article. All significant words in a title are paired, and these pairs are arranged alphabetically as an index to authors. For example, if you were investigating the effect of dyslexia on children's reading ability, the three basic terms would be combined as follows:

Main Term	*Coterm*
Dyslexia	Children
Dyslexia	Reading
Children	Dyslexia
Children	Reading
Reading	Dyslexia
Reading	Children

In the 1982 volume, under DYSLEXIA you would find a series of coterms from ABILITY to YUGOSLAVIA. Under READING you might choose the name M. E. Thomson. If you looked under READING, you would find DYSLEXIA as a coterm and under it five names including M. E. Thomson. Under CHILDREN both READING and DYSLEXIA would be coterms, and Thomson's name would appear under each of them. This index can be most useful when you begin research with a general subject in mind but without the names of any authorities in the field. By looking under your subject and tracing the key words with which it is combined, you can narrow your subject and also identify authors of usable articles. Because titles, especially in the Humanities, are sometimes more fanciful than descriptive, catalogers may "enrich" a title (supply key terms) to identify it.

2. *Source Index.* In this volume, which is arranged by author and resembles other periodical indexes, you could look up M. E. Thomson and find the title of an article, "The Assessment of Children with Specific Reading Difficulties (Dyslexia) Using the British Ability Scales." The next line identifies the source: *British Journal of Psychology,* volume 73, pages 461–78. Below are names of twenty-eight authors who are cited in Thomson's article. Some of these names

might lead you to additional articles if you looked them up in earlier volumes of *Source Index.*

3. ***Citation Index.*** This volume lists the number of times an author or an artist has been cited in works written by others. If you were preparing a paper on Shelley, for example, you might begin with the knowledge that Harold Bloom is an authority on Romantic poetry. By looking in the *Arts & Humanities Citation Index* for 1982, you would find under BLOOM a list of 212 citations. The citations are subdivided, and under SHELLEY'S MYTHMAKING (a book by Bloom), you would find seven names. You could then check those names in the *Source Index* to locate usable articles. If you looked under SHELLEY, you would find two columns of citations, subdivided by titles of his poems. If you were writing on ALASTOR, you would find under that entry the names of authors who referred to that poem in 1982 and then locate their articles in the *Source Index.*

These indexes can be rather intimidating because they contain vast quantities of information (literally, millions of items) and the condensed form of the entries differs from that used in other indexes. However, they can direct you to many sources that you might otherwise overlook. With a little practice, you can master the basic procedures and you will find them a very valuable source of references.

Other Indexes

The format of four other useful indexes is illustrated by the following brief excerpts:

1. ***Biography Index.*** An index to biographical information in books and periodicals. An appendix lists subjects by profession or occupation.

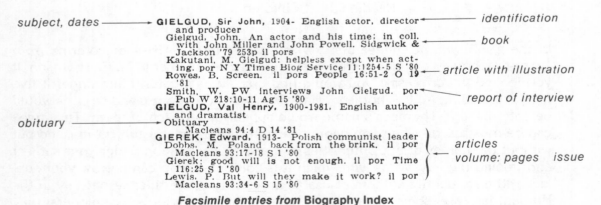

Facsimile entries from Biography Index

2. **Book Review Digest.** A guide to reviews of approximately 6,000 books a year. Entries are arranged by author; a subject and title index follows the main section. The essential information is a book's publication-year; you can learn this from the title page of the book, from the card catalog, or from *Books in Print*.

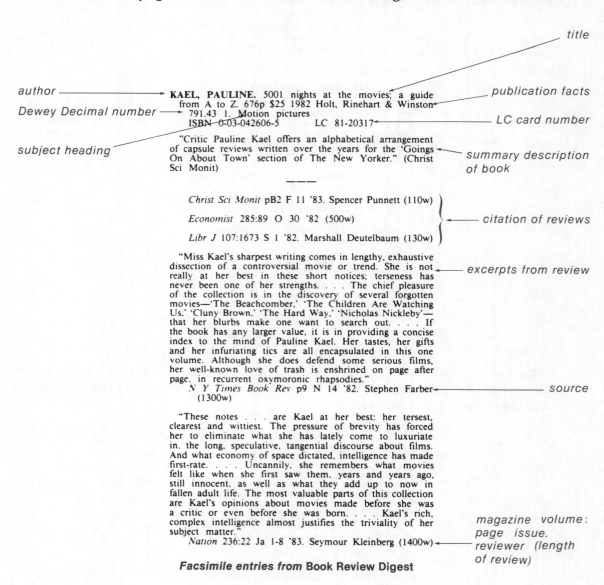

Facsimile entries from Book Review Digest

3. **Essay and General Literature Index.** Especially useful as a guide to anthologies and composite volumes. Literary figures are emphasized, but other subjects are included. The publishers of all books cited are listed in an appendix.

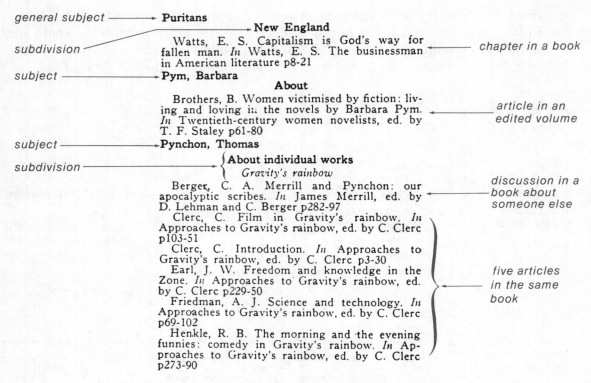

general subject ──────→ **Puritans**

subdivision ─────→ **New England**

Watts, E. S. Capitalism is God's way for fallen man. *In* Watts, E. S. The businessman in American literature p8-21 ──────→ *chapter in a book*

subject ──────→ **Pym, Barbara**

About

Brothers, B. Women victimised by fiction: living and loving in the novels by Barbara Pym. *In* Twentieth-century women novelists, ed. by T. F. Staley p61-80 ──────→ *article in an edited volume*

subject ──────→ **Pynchon, Thomas**

subdivision ──────→ **About individual works**
Gravity's rainbow

Berger, C. A. Merrill and Pynchon: our apocalyptic scribes. *In* James Merrill, ed. by D. Lehman and C. Berger p282-97 ──────→ *discussion in a book about someone else*

Clerc, C. Film in Gravity's rainbow. *In* Approaches to Gravity's rainbow, ed. by C. Clerc p103-51

Clerc, C. Introduction. *In* Approaches to Gravity's rainbow, ed. by C. Clerc p3-30

Earl, J. W. Freedom and knowledge in the Zone. *In* Approaches to Gravity's rainbow, ed. by C. Clerc p229-50

Friedman, A. J. Science and technology. *In* Approaches to Gravity's rainbow, ed. by C. Clerc p69-102

Henkle, R. B. The morning and the evening funnies: comedy in Gravity's rainbow. *In* Approaches to Gravity's rainbow, ed. by C. Clerc p273-90

──────→ *five articles in the same book*

Facsimile entries from Essay and General Literature Index

4. *New York Times Index.* The index of this newspaper is useful for dating events as well as for locating stories. Entries are arranged alphabetically by subject and are lavishly cross-referenced.

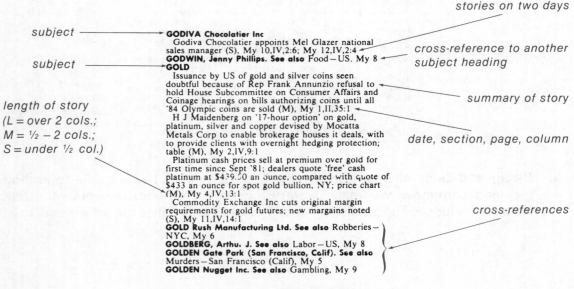

stories on two days

subject ──────→ **GODIVA Chocolatier Inc**
Godiva Chocolatier appoints Mel Glazer national sales manager (S), My 10,IV,2:6; My 12,IV,2:4 ──────

subject ──────→ **GODWIN, Jenny Phillips. See also** Food—US. My 8 ──────→ *cross-reference to another subject heading*

subject ──────→ **GOLD**
Issuance by US of gold and silver coins seen doubtful because of Rep Frank Annunzio refusal to hold House Subcommittee on Consumer Affairs and Coinage hearings on bills authorizing coins until all '84 Olympic coins are sold (M), My 1,II,35:1 ──────→ *summary of story*

length of story (L = over 2 cols.; M = ½ – 2 cols.; S = under ½ col.)

H J Maidenberg on '17-hour option' on gold, platinum, silver and copper devised by Mocatta Metals Corp to enable brokerage houses it deals, with to provide clients with overnight hedging protection; table (M), My 2,IV,9:1 ──────→ *date, section, page, column*

Platinum cash prices sell at premium over gold for first time since Sept '81; dealers quote 'free' cash platinum at $439.50 an ounce, compared with quote of $433 an ounce for spot gold bullion, NY; price chart (M), My 4,IV,13:1

Commodity Exchange Inc cuts original margin requirements for gold futures; new margains noted (S), My 11,IV,14:1

GOLD Rush Manufacturing Ltd. See also Robberies—NYC, My 6

GOLDBERG, Arthu. J. See also Labor—US, My 8

GOLDEN Gate Park (San Francisco, Calif). See also Murders—San Francisco (Calif), My 5

GOLDEN Nugget Inc. See also Gambling, My 9

──────→ *cross-references*

Facsimile entries from New York Times Index

GENERAL REFERENCE WORKS
(Exercise F)

General reference works are most likely to be found in the Reference Room. The listing below probably represents less than five percent of the wealth of reference material available, but it includes sources most frequently used. When you locate one of these works in the Reference Room or in the stacks, look at the volumes beside it; they will be of the same general type and may prove useful.

In the selective bibliography below, a dash after a year (1972—) indicates the continuing publication of a serial. Some lengthy titles have been shortened. American publishers or distributors have been cited whenever possible. Brief comments within parentheses describe special features of some works.

Atlases and Gazetteers

For information about places, you should turn first to an atlas (essentially a collection of maps) or a gazetteer (a dictionary of places). Check the copyright year of such sources to be certain that the information is up-to-date.

Atlas of the Universe. Ed. Patrick Moore. Chicago: Rand McNally, 1970.
Columbia Lippincott Gazetteer of the World. Ed. Leon E. Seltzer. 2nd ed. New York: Columbia Univ. Press, 1962.
Hammond Medallion World Atlas. Maplewood, N.J.: Hammond, 1978.
National Atlas of the United States. Washington, D.C.: Government Printing Office, 1970.
National Geographic Atlas of the World.. 5th ed. Washington, D.C.: National Geographic Society, 1981.
Rand McNally Commercial Atlas and Marketing Guide. New York: Rand McNally, 1976—. (Annually.)
The Times Atlas of the World. Rev. ed. New York: Times Books, 1980.
Webster's New Geographical Dictionary. Rev. ed. Springfield, Mass.: G. & C. Merriam, 1977.

Biography

For a complete account of a public figure's life, use full-length biographies, but for basic biographical data, reference works like those below are indispensable. There is a wide range of specialized biographical references such as *Who's Who in New Zealand* or *Who's Who in Opera.* In *Books in Print* (1982), there are 222 titles beginning with the words "Who's Who."

American Men and Women of Science. 15th ed. 7 vols. New York: Bowker, 1982.
Biography Index. New York: H. W. Wilson, 1947—. (Quarterly. Cumulated annually and every three years. An index to books and articles about living and nonliving persons. See p. 28.)
Current Biography. New York: H. W. Wilson, 1940—. (Monthly except August. Articles about living persons. Especially useful for current celebrities. Index in each annual volume covers preceding years in the decade.)
Dictionary of American Biography. 20 vols. New York: Scribner's, 1928—. (Index. Supplements. Authoritative articles on Americans no longer living who have made significant contributions to American life.)
Dictionary of National Biography. 63 vols. London: Smith, Elder, 1885—. (Supplements. The basic source of biographical information about English notables no longer living.)
The McGraw-Hill Encyclopedia of World Biography. 12 vols. New York: McGraw-Hill, 1973.
National Cyclopaedia of American Biography. 60 vols. Clifton, N.J.: T. White, 1892—. (Supplements. Includes living and deceased persons. Not alphabetized; consult index.)

Webster's Biographical Dictionary. 3rd ed. Springfield, Mass.: G. & C. Merriam, 1976.
Who's Who. London: Black, 1849—. (Annually. *Who Was Who* reprints discontinued entries.)
Who's Who in America. Chicago: Marquis, 1899—. (Biennially. *Who Was Who in America* reprints discontinued entries.)

Dictionaries

For spelling, capitalization, and such information, you can use any standard desk dictionary. For precise shades of meaning and a wider range of synonyms, use an unabridged dictionary. For the semantic history of a word, use a historical dictionary (*OED* or *DAE*).

A Dictionary of American English on Historical Principles. 4 vols. Chicago: Univ. of Chicago Press, 1936–44. (*DAE.* A historical dictionary of American words and meanings modeled after the *OED.*)
Funk & Wagnalls New Standard Dictionary of the English Language. New York: Funk & Wagnalls, 1964.
A New English Dictionary on Historical Principles. 10 vols. Oxford: Clarendon Press, 1884–1933. (Generally referred to as *OED* since 1933 when reissued as *The Oxford English Dictionary.* 13 vols. Dated illustrative quotations trace the history of a word's meanings. Three-volume supplement underway.)
Random House Dictionary of the English Language. 2nd ed. New York: Random House, 1968.
Webster's Third New International Dictionary of the English Language. Springfield, Mass.: G & C. Merriam, 1961. (Often referred to as W 3.)

Dictionaries of Quotations

Works like those listed below are useful when you need to discover or verify the source of a quotation. Because the methods of organization vary, it is helpful to look over the preface before using a volume.

Dictionary of Quotations. Ed. Bergen Evans. New York: Delacorte, 1968. (Arranged alphabetically by subject.)
Familiar Quotations. Ed. John Bartlett. 15th ed. Boston: Little, Brown, 1980. (Arranged chronologically by author. Index.)
The Home Book of Quotations, Classical and Modern. Ed. Burton E. Stevenson. 10th ed. New York: Dodd, Mead, 1967. (Arranged by subject. Key-word index.)
The International Thesaurus of Quotations. Ed. Rhoda T. Tripp. New York: Crowell, 1970. (Entries arranged in "idea groups.")
New Cyclopedia of Practical Quotations. Ed. Jehiel K. Hoyt. New York: Somerset Books, 1947. (Arranged by subject. Index.)
A New Dictionary of Quotations. Ed. Henry L. Mencken. New York: Knopf, 1942. (Arranged by subject. No index.)
Oxford Dictionary of Quotations. 3rd ed. New York: Oxford Univ. Press, 1979. (Arranged alphabetically by author.)

Encyclopedias

Encyclopedias are particularly useful for finding specific factual information and for exploratory reading while you are narrowing a topic. The starred encyclopedias follow a policy of "continuous revision," in which articles are brought up to date annually. Encyclopedias are usually identified by year (1984 ed.) rather than by number (14th ed.).

Collier's Encyclopedia. 24 vols. New York: Colliers. (Designed for high school and college use. Supplement, *Collier's Encyclopedia Yearbook.*)

Encyclopaedia Britannica. 24 vols. Chicago: Encyclopaedia Britannica. (Index and atlas in final volume. Traditionally strong in history and literature. Superseded by the 15th edition, described below, but still useful.)

Encyclopaedia Britannica. 30 vols. 15th ed. Chicago: Encyclopaedia Britannica. (In 1974 the *Britannica* was completely restructured into three parts: *Micropaedia,* 10 vols., containing short factual articles; *Macropaedia,* 19 vols., containing over 4,000 in-depth articles; and *Propaedia*, an outline of knowledge serving as an index to the other 29 volumes.)

Encyclopaedia of the Social Sciences. 15 vols. New York: Macmillan, 1930–35.

Encyclopedia Americana. 30 vols. New York: Americana Corp. (Especially strong in science and technology. Supplement, *Americana Annual.*)

The New Columbia Encyclopedia. 4th ed. New York: Columbia Univ. Press, 1975.

Van Nostrand's Scientific Encyclopedia. 6th ed. 2 vols. New York: Van Nostrand Reinhold, 1976. (Useful for definitions and basic information in all scientific fields.)

Government Publications

The vast number of reports, pamphlets, maps, and other material published by the U.S. Government makes reference works like the following indispensable. (See pp. 57–58.)

American Statistics Index. Washington, D.C.: Congressional Information Service, 1973—. (Annually. Monthly supplements. Index and abstracts of all government publications containing statistical data.)

Congressional Information Service Index to Publications of the United States Congress. Washington, D.C.: Congressional Information Service, 1970—. (Useful for hearings and other activities of Congressional committees. Brief abstracts. Monthly. Annual cumulations. Known as *CIS/Index.*)

Guide to U.S. Government Publications. McLean, Va.: Documents Index, 1973—. (Annually. Quarterly supplements.)

Leidy, William P. *A Popular Guide to Government Publications.* 4th ed. New York: Columbia Univ. Press, 1976.

Monthly Catalog of U.S. Government Publications. Washington, D.C.: Government Printing Office, 1895. (Monthly issues. Index.)

Monthly Checklist of State Publications. Washington, D.C.: Government Printing Office, 1910—. (Monthly. Annual cumulations.)

Pohle, Linden. *A Guide to Popular Government Publications.* Littleton, Colo.: Libraries Unlimited, 1972.

Schmeckebier, Laurence F., and Roy B. Eastin. *Government Publications and Their Use.* Washington, D.C.: Brookings Institution, 1969.

Vertical File Index. New York: H. W. Wilson, 1935—. (Monthly except August. Lists pamphlets and booklets by subject. Annual index of titles.)

Indexes

Just as the index of a book does not discuss a subject but indicates where a discussion can be found, a reference work called an index will direct you to sources. Indexes to periodicals are especially useful. Most follow the basic format of *Readers' Guide.* (See pp. 24–26.)

Applied Science and Technology Index. New York: H. W. Wilson, 1958—. (Formerly *Industrial Arts Index,* 1913–57. Subject index. Monthly except July. Quarterly and annual cumulations.)

Arts & Humanities Citation Index. Philadelphia: Institute for Scientific Information, 1978—. (Indexes periodicals and books. Two quarterly volumes a year and an annual volume. See pp. 27–28.)

Biographical Dictionaries: Master Index. 3 vols. Detroit: Gale, 1975. (An index to biographical information in more than fifty sources. Two supplementary volumes, 1979–80.)

Book Review Digest. New York: H. W. Wilson, 1905—. (Monthly except February and July. Annual cumulations. Title and subject index. Digests of many book reviews and citations of others. See p. 29.)

Encyclopedia of Associations. Detroit: Gale, 1956—. (Biennial. Brief descriptions of national and international organizations of all types.)

Essay and General Literature Index. New York: H. W. Wilson, 1934—.(Author–subject index of books, especially useful for anthologies. The first volume covers 1900–33. See pp. 29–30.)

Humanities Index. New York: H. W. Wilson, 1974—. (Quarterly. Annual cumulations. Supersedes *International Index,* 1907–65, and *Social Sciences & Humanities Index,* 1965–74.)

Index to Book Reviews in the Humanities. Detroit: Phillip Thomson, 1960—. (Quarterly. Annual cumulations.)

Magazine Index. Menlo Park, Calif.: Information Access, 1976—.(Monthly index of more than 400 American magazines. Available only on microfilm and online computer. Dialog.)

National Newspaper Index. Menlo Park, Calif.: Information Access, 1979—. (Indexes *New York Times, Christian Science Monitor,* and *Wall Street Journal.* Monthly updates. Microfilm and online computer. Dialog.)

New York Times Index. New York: New York Times, 1913—. (Subject index. Summaries of news items. Useful for dating an event even when the newspaper is not available. Semimonthly. Annual cumulations. Quarterly cumulations since 1978. See p. 30.)

Nineteenth Century Readers' Guide. 2 vols. New York: H. W. Wilson, 1944. (Indexes periodicals from 1890 to 1899 and includes entries omitted from *Readers' Guide,* 1900–22.)

Poole's Index to Periodical Literature. 6 vols. Boston: Houghton Mifflin, 1888–1908. (Subject index. Stories and poems are listed by title. Indexes periodicals from 1802 to 1906.)

Public Affairs Information Service. New York: Public Affairs Information Service, 1915—. (Subject index to periodicals, pamphlets, and some books. Weekly. Bimonthly and annual cumulations.)

Readers' Guide to Periodical Literature. New York: H. W. Wilson, 1905—. (Semimonthly, monthly in July and August. Quarterly, annual, and biennial cumulations. Indexes general interest periodicals from 1900 to the present. See pp. 24–26.)

Science Citation Index. Philadelphia: Institute for Scientific Information, 1961—. (Index to periodicals and some books. Two quarterly volumes, annual and five-year cumulations. See pp. 27–28.)

Social Sciences Citation Index. Philadelphia: Institute for Scientific Information, 1972—. (Index to periodicals and books. Two quarterly volumes, annual and five-year cumulations. See pp. 27–28.)

Social Sciences Index. New York: H. W. Wilson, 1974—. (Quarterly. Annual cumulations. Supersedes *Social Sciences and Humanities Index,* 1965–74.)

Technical Book Review Index. Pittsburgh: Carnegie Library, 1917–29, 1935—. (Monthly except July and August. Annual cumulations.)

Yearbooks

Yearbooks, almanacs, and handbooks are a useful source of statistics and similar factual data. In most you must first consult the index.

An Almanack. London: Whitaker, 1869—. (Generally known as *Whitaker's Almanack.*)

Annual Register of World Events: A Review of the Year. New York: St. Martin's, 1758—.

Europa Year Book. 2 vols. London: Europa, 1959—. (Factual data on European countries in first volume, on other countries in second.)

Facts on File. New York: Facts on File, 1940—. (Weekly news digests. Annual cumulation entitled *News Dictionary.*)

Guinness Book of World Records. New York: Sterling, 1962—. (Annual compilations of records in almost every human activity.)

Information Please Almanac. New York: Simon and Schuster, 1947—.

Keesing's Contemporary Archives. London: Keesing's, 1931—. (Weekly news digests. Biennial cumulations.)

Statesman's Yearbook. New York: St. Martin's Press, 1864—. (A British handbook. Useful for information on governments and international organizations.)

Statistical Abstract of the United States. Washington, D.C.: Government Printing Office, 1878—. (Annual summary of statistics prepared by the Bureau of the Census.)

The World Almanac and Book of Facts. New York: Newspaper Enterprise Assn., 1868—. (Useful for statistics and similar facts.)

SPECIALIZED REFERENCE WORKS

Some basic reference sources in eighteen academic disciplines are listed below.

Art	Film	Physics
Biology	History	Political Science
Business	Literature	Psychology
Chemistry	Music	Religion
Economics	Mythology and Folklore	Sociology
Education	Philosophy	Women's Studies

Periodicals are not included because there are literally thousands of them, from special-topics newsletters to major journals. In gathering material, your concern should be to find specific articles rather than entire magazines, and so your most important resource will be the general periodical indexes listed above and the specialized indexes listed below.

Art

Arntzen, Etta Mae, and Robert Rainwater. *Guide to the Literature of Art History.* Chicago: American Library Assn., 1980.

Art Index. New York: H. W. Wilson, 1929—. (Author–subject index to periodicals. Quarterly. Annual and biennial cumulations.)

Arts in America: A Bibliography. 4 vols. Ed. Bernard Karpel. Washington, D.C.: Smithsonian Institution, 1979.

Canaday, John E. *Lives of the Painters.* 4 vols. New York: Norton, 1969.

Dictionary of Contemporary American Artists. Ed. Paul Cummings. 3rd ed. New York: St. Martin's Press, 1977.

Encyclopedia of World Art. 15 vols. New York: McGraw-Hill, 1959–68.

Gardner, Helen. *Gardner's Art through the Ages.* 7th ed. 2 vols. New York: Harcourt Brace, 1980. (A basic source, revisions by various editors.)

Groce, George C., and David H. Wallace. *The New York Historical Society's Dictionary of Artists in America, 1564–1860.* New Haven, Conn.: Yale Univ. Press, 1957.

Index of Twentieth Century Artists. 4 vols. New York: College Art Assn., 1933–37. (Rpt. Arno Press, 1970.)

Janson, Horst W., and Dora Jane Janson. *History of Art.* 2nd ed. New York: H. N. Abrams, 1977.

Larkin, Oliver W. *Art and Life in America.* Rev. ed. New York: Holt, 1960.

Lucas, E. Louise. *Art Books: A Basic Bibliography in the Fine Arts.* Greenwich, Conn.: New York Graphic Society, 1968.

Mayer, Ralph. *A Dictionary of Art Terms and Techniques.* New York: Lewis, 1981.

The Oxford Companion to Art. Ed. Harold Osborne. New York: Oxford Univ. Press, 1970.

Robb, David M., and Jessie J. Garrison. *Art in the Western World.* 4th ed. New York: Harper, 1963.

Sturgis, Rusell. *Dictionary of Architecture and Building.* 3 vols. New York: Macmillan, 1901. (Rpt. Gale, 1966.)

Walker, John Albert. *Glossary of Art, Architecture and Design Since 1945.* 2nd rev. ed. Hamden, Conn.: Linnet Books, 1977.

Biology

Biological Abstracts. Philadelphia: Biological Abstracts, 1926—.(Semimonthly. Annual cumulations.)

Biological and Agricultural Index. New York: H. W. Wilson, 1964—.(Supersedes *Agricultural Index,* 1916–64. Subject index. Monthly except August. Annual cumulations.)

Bottle, Robert T., and H. V. Wyatt. *The Use of Biological Literature.* 2nd ed. Hamden, Conn.: Archon, 1971.

The Encyclopedia of the Biological Sciences. Ed. Peter Gray. 2nd. ed. New York: Van Nostrand Reinhold, 1970.

Henderson, Isabella F., and William D. Henderson. *A Dictionary of Biological Terms.* 8th ed. Princeton, N.J.: Van Nostrand Reinhold, 1963.

Jaeger, Edmund C. *A Source-book of Biological Names and Terms.* 3rd ed. Springfield, Ill.: Thomas, 1978.

Leftwich, A. W. *A Dictionary of Zoology.* 3rd ed. New York: Van Nostrand Reinhold, 1973.

Walker, Ernest P., and others. *Mammals of the World.* 3rd ed. 2 vols. Baltimore: Johns Hopkins Univ. Press, 1975.

Willis, J. C. *A Dictionary of the Flowering Plants and Ferns.* 8th ed. New York: Cambridge Univ. Press, 1973.

Business

Accountants' Index. New York: American Institute of C.P.A.'s, 1921—. (Quarterly. Annual cumulations.)

Ammer, Christine, and Dean S. Ammer. *Dictionary of Business and Economics.* New York: Free Press, 1977.

Bibliographic Guide to Business and Economics. Boston: G. K. Hall, 1975—. (Annual bibliographies.)

Bogen, Jules I., and S. S. Shipman. *Financial Handbook.* 4th ed. New York: Wiley, 1968.

Business Periodicals Index. New York: H. W. Wilson, 1958—. (Supersedes *Industrial Arts Index,* 1913–57. Subject index. Monthly except August. Annual cumulations.)

Commodity Year Book. New York: Commodity Research Bureau, 1939—.(Annual volumes except for 1943–47.)

Daniells, Lorna M. *Business Information Sources.* Berkeley: Univ. of California Press, 1976.

Dictionary of Economics and Business. Ed. Erwin E. Nemmers. 4th ed. Totowa, N.J.: Littlefield, 1978.

Encyclopedic Dictionary of Business Finance. Englewood Cliffs, N.J.: Prentice-Hall, 1961.

Kohler, Eric L. *A Dictionary for Accountants.* 5th ed. Englewood Cliffs, N.J.: Prentice-Hall, 1975.

Kraus, Albert L. *The New York Times Guide to Busines and Finance.* New York: Harper and Row, 1972.

Munn, Glenn G. *Encyclopedia of Banking and Finance.* Ed. Ferdinand L. Garcia. 7th ed. Boston: Bankers Publishing, 1973.

Poor's Register of Corporations, Directors and Executives. New York: Standard and Poor's, 1928—. (Annually.)

Wyckoff, Peter. *The Language of Wall Street.* New York: Hopkinson & Blake, 1973.

Chemistry

Chemical Abstracts. Columbus, Ohio: American Chemical Society, 1907—.(Semimonthly. Indexed annually and every ten years.)

The Condensed Chemical Dictionary. Ed. Gessner G. Hawley. 10th ed. New York: Van Nostrand Reinhold, 1981.

Crane, Evan Jay, and others. *A Guide to the Literature of Chemistry.* 2nd ed. New York: Wiley, 1957.

Encyclopedia of Chemistry. Eds. Clifford A. Hampel and Gessner G. Hawley. 3rd ed. New York: Van Nostrand Reinhold, 1973.

Handbook of Chemistry and Physics. Cleveland: Chemical Rubber Co., 1913—. (Annual revisions.)

Maizell, Robert E. How to Find Chemical Information. New York: Wiley, 1979.

Mellon, Melvin G. Chemical Publications: Their Nature and Use. 5th ed. New York: McGraw-Hill, 1982.

Thorpe, Jocelyn F., and M. A. Whiteley. Thorpe's Dictionary of Applied Chemistry. 4th ed. 12 vols. New York: Longman's, 1937–56.

The Use of Chemical Literature. Ed. Robert T. Bottle. 3rd ed. Boston: Butterworth, 1979.

Woodburn, Henry M. Using the Chemical Literature. New York: Marcel Dekker, 1974.

Economics

Amstutz, Mark R. Economics and Foreign Policy: A Guide to Information Sources. Detroit: Gale, 1977.

Bibliographic Guide to Business and Economics. Boston: G. K. Hall, 1975—. (Annually.)

Fletcher, John. The Uses of Economic Literature. Hamden, Conn.: Archon, 1971.

Hanson, John L. A Dictionary of Economics and Commerce. 5th ed. Plymouth, England: MacDonald & Evans, 1977.

McGraw-Hill Dictionary of Modern Economics. 2nd ed. New York: McGraw-Hill, 1973.

Moffat, Donald W. Economics Dictionary. New York: Elsevier, 1976.

Sloan, Harold S., and Arnold J. Zurcher. Dictionary of Economics. 5th ed. New York: Barnes & Noble, 1971.

Education

Altbach, Philip G. Comparative Higher Education Abroad: Bibliography and Analysis. New York: Praeger, 1976.

Berry, Dorothy M. A Bibliographical Guide to Educational Research. Metuchen, N.J.: Scarecrow Press, 1975.

Best, John W. Research in Education. 4th ed. Englewood Cliffs, N.J.: Prentice-Hall, 1981.

Current Index to Journals in Education. New York, Macmillan, 1969—.(Monthly. Semiannual and annual indexes.)

Dictionary of Education. Ed. Carter V. Good. 3rd ed. New York: McGraw-Hill, 1973.

Education Index. New York: H. W. Wilson, 1929—. (Author–subject index. Monthly except July and August. Annual cumulations.)

Encyclopedia of Education. 10 vols. New York: Macmillan, 1971.

Encyclopedia of Educational Research. Ed. Harold Mitzel. 4 vols. New York: Macmillan, 1969.

International Dictionary of Education. Eds. G. Terry Page and others. New York: Nichols, 1977.

Leaders in Education. 5th ed. New York: R. R. Bowker and Jacques Cattell Press, 1974.

Resources in Education. Washington, D.C.: National Institute of Education, 1976—. (Sponsored by Educational Resources Information Center, ERIC. Monthly indexes and abstracts. Indexes cumulated semiannually as Research in Education. See pp. 25, 27.)

Woodbury, Marda. A Guide to Sources of Educational Information. Washington, D.C.: Information Resources Press, 1976.

Film

Armour, Robert A. Film: A Reference Guide. Westport, Conn.: Greenwood Press, 1980.

Bukalski, Peter J. Film Research: A Critical Bibliography. Boston: G. K. Hall, 1972.

Film Literature Index. New York: Filmdex, 1973—. (Subject–author index. Quarterly. Annual cumulations.)

Film Review Digest. Millwood, N.Y.: Kraus-Thomson, 1975—. (Quarterly. Annual cumulations.)

Geduld, Harry M., and Ronald Gottesman. An Illustrated Glossary of Film Terms. New York: Holt, Rinehart, 1973.

Halliwell, Leslie. *The Filmgoer's Companion.* 6th ed. New York: Hill & Wang, 1977.
International Encyclopedia of Film. Ed. Roger Manvell. New York: Crown, 1972.
International Index to Film Periodicals. New York: Bowker, 1972—.(Annually.)
International Motion Picture Almanac. New York: Quigley, 1929—.
Manchel, Frank. *Film Study: A Resource Guide.* Rutherford, N.J.: Fairleigh Dickinson Univ. Press, 1973.
New York Times Film Reviews 1913–1968. 6 vols. New York: New York Times and Arno Press, 1970.
The Oxford Companion to Film. Ed. Liz-Anne Bawden. New York: Oxford Univ. Press, 1976.
Sheahan, Eileen. *Moving Pictures.* South Brunswick, N.J.: A. S. Barnes, 1979. (Annotated bibliography.)

History

America: History and Life. Santa Barbara, Calif.: ABC-Clio Press, 1964—. (Abstracts, book reviews, bibliographies. Three issues a year.)
Beers, Henry P. *Bibliographies in American History.* Rev. ed. New York: H. W. Wilson, 1942. (Rpt. Octagon, 1973.)
Cambridge Ancient History. 12 vols. New York: Cambridge Univ. Press, 1923–39. (Revision in progress.)
Cambridge Medieval History. 8 vols. New York: Cambridge Univ. Press, 1911–36. (Revision in progress.)
Cartwright, William H., and Richard L. Watson, Jr. *The Reinterpretation of American History and Culture.* Washington, D.C.: National Council for the Social Studies, 1973.
Commager, Henry S. *Documents of American History.* 2 vols. 9th ed. New York: Appleton-Century-Crofts, 1973.
Day, Alan E. *History: A Reference Handbook.* Hamden, Conn.: Linnet Books, 1977.
Dictionary of American History. Rev. ed. 8 vols. New York: Scribner's, 1976.
An Encyclopedia of World History: Ancient, Medieval and Modern. 5th ed. Boston: Houghton Mifflin, 1972.
Guide to Historical Literature. New York: Macmillan, 1961.
A Guide to Historical Method. Ed. Robert J. Shafer. 3rd ed. Homewood, Ill.: Dorsey Press, 1980.
Harvard Guide to American History. Eds. Frank Freidel and Richard K. Showman. Rev. ed. 2 vols. Cambridge, Mass.: Harvard Univ. Press, 1974.
Historical Abstracts, 1775–1945. Santa Barbara, Calif.: ABC-Clio Press, 1955—. (Quarterly. Cumulative index every five years.)
Historical Atlas of Britain. Eds. Malcolm Falkus and John Gillingham. New York: Continuum, 1981.
Howat, G. M. D. *Dictionary of World History.* New York: Thomas Nelson, 1973.
Index to Book Reviews in Historical Periodicals. Metuchen, N.J.: Scarecrow Press, 1972—. (Annually.)
Keller, Helen R. *Dictionary of Dates.* 2 vols. New York: Macmillan, 1934.
Morris, Richard B. *Encyclopedia of American History.* 5th ed. New York: Harper and Row, 1976.
New Cambridge Modern History. 14 vols. New York: Cambridge Univ. Press, 1957–70. (Revision of 1902–26 edition.)
Poulton, Helen J. *The Historian's Handbook.* Norman, Okla.: Univ. of Oklahoma Press, 1977.
Roach, John P. C. *A Bibliography of Modern History.* New York: Cambridge Univ. Press, 1968.
Stephens, Lester D. *Historiography: A Bibliography.* Metuchen, N.J.: Scarecrow Press, 1975.

Literature

Abstracts of English Studies. Urbana, Ill.: National Council of Teachers of English, 1958—. (Ten issues a year.)
American Authors, 1600–1900. Eds. Stanley J. Kunitz and Howard Haycraft. New York: H. W. Wilson, 1938.
American Literary Scholarship. Durham, N.C.: Duke Univ. Press, 1963—.(Annually. Useful bibliographical essays.)
Articles on American Literature, 1900–1950. Ed. Lewis G. Leary. Durham, N.C.: Duke Univ. Press, 1954. (Two additional volumes cover the years 1950–75.)
Author Biographies Master Index. 2 vols. Detroit: Gale, 1978. (Index of biographical dictionaries.)

Baker, Ernest A. *A History of the English Novel.* 11 vols. London: Witherby, 1924–39. (Rpt. Barnes & Noble, 1950.)

Barzun, Jacques, and Wendell Hertig. *A Catalogue of Crime.* New York: Harper and Row, 1971. (Biographical and bibliographical information on detective fiction.)

Benet, William R. *The Reader's Encyclopedia.* 2nd ed. New York: Crowell, 1965.

Black American Writers, Past and Present: A Biographical and Bibliographical Dictionary. Eds. Theressa G. Rush and others. 2 vols. Metuchen, N.J.: Scarecrow Press, 1975.

Black American Writers, 1773–1949: A Bibliography and Union List. Ed. Geraldine O. Matthews. Boston: G. K. Hall, 1975.

Blanck, Jacob N. *Bibliography of American Literature.* 6 vols. New Haven, Conn.: Yale Univ. Press, 1955–73.

Briney, Robert E., and Edward Wood. *SF Bibliographies.* Chicago: Advent, 1972.

Cambridge History of American Literature. 4 vols. New York: Putnam, 1917–21. (Bibliography in each volume.)

Cambridge History of English Literature. 15 vols. New York: Putnam, 1907–33. (Bibliography in each volume.)

Columbia Dictionary of Modern European Literature. New York: Columbia Univ. Press, 1947.

Gohdes, Clarence. *Bibliographical Guide to the Study of Literature of the U.S.A.* 4th ed. Durham, N.C.: Duke Univ. Press, 1976.

Hackett, Alice Payne, and James H. Burke. *80 Years of Best Sellers, 1895–1975.* New York: R. R. Bowker, 1977.

Holman, C. Hugh. *A Handbook to Literature.* 3rd ed. Indianapolis: Odyssey Press, 1972. (Thorough revision of a standard reference work with the same title by Thrall and Hibbard.)

A Literary History of England. Ed. Albert C. Baugh. 2nd ed. 4 vols. Englewood Cliffs, N.J.: Prentice-Hall, 1967.

MLA International Bibliography. New York: Modern Language Assn., 1921—. (The most complete annual bibliography. International coverage and the present title began in 1956.)

New Cambridge Bibliography of English Literature. 5 vols. New York: Cambridge Univ. Press, 1969–77.

New Century Classical Handbook. New York: Appleton-Century-Crofts, 1962.

New York Theatre Reviews, 1870–1919. 6 vols. New York: New York Times and Arno Press, 1975.

New York Theatre Reviews, 1920–1970. 10 vols. New York: New York Times, 1971.

The Oxford Companion to American Literature. Ed. James D. Hart. 4th ed. New York: Oxford Univ. Press, 1965.

The Oxford Companion to Classical Literature. Ed. Sir Paul Harvey. Rev. ed. New York: Oxford Univ. Press, 1966.

The Oxford Companion to English Literature. Ed. Sir Paul Harvey. 4th ed. New York: Oxford Univ. Press, 1967.

Oxford History of English Literature. 12 vols. New York: Oxford Univ. Press, 1945—. (In progress.)

Science Fiction Book Review Index, 1923–1973. Ed. Halbert W. Hall. Detroit: Gale, 1975. (A second volume covers the years 1974–79, and annual supplements are planned.)

The Science Fiction Encyclopedia. Ed. Peter Nicholls. Garden City, N.Y.: Doubleday, 1979.

Spiller, Robert E., and others. *Literary History of the United States.* 4th ed. 3 vols. New York: Macmillan, 1974.

Twentieth-Century American Science Fiction Writers. 2 vols. Detroit: Gale, 1981.

Twentieth Century Authors. Eds. Stanley J. Kunitz and Howard Haycraft. New York: H. W. Wilson, 1942. (Supplement, 1955.)

Music

Abraham, Gerald E. H. *The Concise Oxford History of Music.* New York: Oxford Univ. Press, 1979.

Anderson, Ruth. *Contemporary American Composers: A Biographical Dictionary.* Boston: G. K. Hall, 1976.

Apel, Willi. *Harvard Dictionary of Music.* 2nd ed. Cambridge, Mass.: Harvard Univ. Press, 1969.

Baker, Theodore, and Nicolas Slonimsky. *Baker's Biographical Dictionary of Musicians.* 6th ed. New York: Schirmer, 1978.

Barlow, Harold, and Sam Morganstern. *A Dictionary of Musical Themes.* Rev. ed. New York: Crown, 1975.

Blom, Eric. *Everyman's Dictionary of Music.* New York: St. Martin's Press, 1971.

Davies, J. H. *Musicalia: Sources of Information in Music.* 2nd ed. Elmsford, N.Y.: Pergamon, 1969.

Duckles, Vincent H. *Music Reference and Research Materials.* 3rd ed. New York: Free Press, 1974.

Grout, Donald Jay. *A Short History of Opera.* 2nd ed. New York: Columbia Univ. Press, 1965.

The International Cyclopedia of Music and Musicians. Ed. Oscar Thompson. 10th ed. New York: Dodd, Mead, 1975.

Kinkle, Roger D. *The Complete Encyclopedia of Popular Music and Jazz 1900–1950.* 4 vols. New Rochelle, N.Y.: Arlington, 1974.

New College Encyclopedia of Music. Eds. J. A. Westrup and F. L. Harrison. New York: Norton, 1976.

The New Grove Dictionary of Music and Musicians. Ed. Stanley Sadie. 6th ed. 10 vols. Washington, D.C.: Grove's Dictionaries of Music, 1980.

Oxford History of Music. Ed. William H. Hadow. 2nd ed. 8 vols. London: Oxford Univ. Press, 1929–38.

Picerno, Vincent J. *Dictionary of Musical Terms.* Brooklyn, N.Y.: Haskell, 1976.

Scholes, Percy A. *The Oxford Companion to Music.* Ed. John O. Ward. 10th ed. New York: Oxford Univ. Press, 1970.

Watanabe, Ruth T. *Introduction to Music Research.* Englewood Cliffs, N.J.: Prentice-Hall, 1967.

Mythology and Folklore

Abstracts of Folklore Studies. Austin, Tex.: American Folklore Society, 1963—. (Quarterly.)

Brunvand, Jan Harold. *Folklore: A Handbook for Study and Research.* New York: St. Martin's Press, 1976.

Diehl, Katherine S. *Religions, Mythologies, Folklores: An Annotated Bibliography.* 2nd ed. Metuchen, N.J.: Scarecrow Press, 1962.

Frazer, Sir James. *The Golden Bough.* 3rd ed. 12 vols. New York: St. Martin's Press, 1955.

Funk & Wagnall's Standard Dictionary of Folklore, Mythology, and Legend. Ed. Maria Leach. New York: Funk & Wagnalls, 1973. (Reissue of two-volume edition published 1949–50.)

Hamilton, Edith. *Mythology.* Boston: Little, Brown, 1942.

Haywood, Charles. *A Bibliography of North American Folklore and Folksong.* 2nd ed. 2 vols. New York: Dover, 1961.

Mythology of All Races. 13 vols. Boston: Archaeological Institute, 1916–32.

Radford, Edwin, and Mona Radford. *Encyclopaedia of Superstitions.* Rev. ed. Chester Springs, Pa.: Dufour Editions, 1969.

Thompson, Stith. *Motif-Index of Folk-Literature.* Rev. ed. 6 vols. Bloomington, Ind.: Indiana Univ. Press, 1955–58.

Thorndike, Lynn. *A History of Magic and Experimental Science.* 8 vols. New York: Columbia Univ. Press, 1934–58.

Philosophy

Baldwin, James M. *Dictionary of Philosophy and Psychology.* 3 vols. New York: Macmillan, 1901–05. (Bibliography in third volume. Useful though out of date. Rpt. New York: Gordon, 1977.)

Bertman, Martin A. *A Research Guide in Philosophy.* Morristown, N.J.: General Learning Press, 1974.

Borchardt, Dietrich H. *How To Find Out in Philosophy and Psychology.* Elmsford, N.Y.: Pergamon, 1968.

The Concise Encyclopedia of Western Philosophy and Philosophers. Ed. James O. Urmson. 2nd ed. London: Hutchinson, 1975.

Copleston, Frederick. *A History of Philosphy.* 9 vols. Garden City, N.Y.: Doubleday, 1977.

Dictionary of the History of Ideas. 5 vols. New York: Scribner's, 1973–74.

The Encyclopedia of Philosophy. 8 vols. New York: Macmillan, 1967.

Lacey, Alan R. *A Dictionary of Philosophy.* London: Routledge & Kegan Paul, 1976.

New Dictionary of Existentialism. Ed. St. Elmo Nauman, Jr. New York: Philosophical Library, 1971.

Philosopher's Index. Bowling Green, Ohio: Bowling Green Univ. Press, 1967—. (Quarterly author–subject index to periodicals.)

Physics

Concise Dictionary of Physics. Ed. J. Thewlis. Elmsford, N.Y.: Pergamon, 1973.
The Encyclopedia of Physics. Ed. Robert Besancon. 2nd ed. New York: Van Nostrand Reinhold, 1974.
Encyclopedia of Physics. Reading, Mass.: Addison-Wesley, 1981.
Encyclopaedic Dictionary of Physics. Ed. J. Thewlis. 9 vols. Elmsford, N.Y.: Pergamon, 1961–64. (Supplements.)
Handbook of Chemistry and Physics. Cleveland: Chemical Rubber Co., 1913—. (Annual revisions.)
A New Dictionary of Physics. Eds. Harold J. Gray and Alan Isaacs. New York: Longman, 1975.
Parke, Nathan G. *Guide to the Literature of Mathematics and Physics.* 2nd ed. New York: Dover, 1958.
Science Abstracts. London: Institute of Electrical Engineers, 1898—.(Semimonthly. Semiannual author–subject index.)
Whitford, R. H. *Physics Literature: A Reference Manual.* 2nd ed. Metuchen, N.J.: Scarecrow Press, 1968.

Political Science

The Book of the States. Chicago: Council of State Governments, 1935—. (Biennially.)
Brock, Clifton. *The Literature of Political Science.* New York: Bowker, 1969.
Congressional Record, 1873—. (Daily. Cumulated for each session. Annual index. See p. 118.)
A Dictionary of Politics. Ed. Walter Z. Laqueur. Rev. ed. New York: Free Press, 1974.
Garson, G. David. *Handbook of Political Science Methods.* 2nd ed. Boston: Holbrook, 1976.
Greenstein, Fred I., and Nelson W. Polsby. *Handbook of Political Science.* 9 vols. Reading, Mass.: Addison-Wesley, 1975. (Bibliographic essays.)
Holler, Frederick L. *The Information Sources of Political Science.* 2nd ed. 5 vols. Santa Barbara, Calif.: ABC-Clio Press, 1975.
Pfaltzgraff, Robert L. *The Study of International Relations: A Guide to Information Sources.* Detroit: Gale, 1977.
Plano, Jack C., and Milton Greenberg. *The American Political Dictionary.* 5th ed. New York: Holt, Rinehart, 1979.
Political Handbook of the World. New York: McGraw-Hill, 1975—.(Annual revisions. Entitled *Political Handbook and Atlas of the World, 1927–74.*)
Roberts, G. K. *Dictionary of Political Analysis.* New York: St. Martin's Press, 1971.
Smith, Edward C., and Arnold J. Zurcher. *Dictionary of American Politics.* 2nd ed. New York: Barnes & Noble, 1968.
Vose, Clement E. *A Guide to Library Sources in Political Science: American Government.* Washington, D.C.: American Political Science Assn., 1975.
Yearbook of the United Nations. New York: United Nations, 1947—.

Psychology

American Handbook of Psychiatry. Ed. Silvano Arieti. 2nd ed. 6 vols. New York: Basic Books, 1975.
Annual Review of Psychology. Palo Alto, Calif.: Annual Reviews, 1950—.
Bachrach, Arthur J. *Psychological Research: An Introduction.* 4th ed. New York: Random House, 1981.
Bell, James E. *A Guide to Library Research in Psychology.* Dubuque, Iowa: W. C. Brown, 1971.
Drever, James A. *A Dictionary of Psychology.* Rev. ed. Santa Fe, N.M.: Gannon, 1971.
Encyclopedia of Mental Health. 6 vols. New York: Franklin Watts, 1963.
Encyclopedia of Psychoanalysis. Ed. Ludwig Eidelberg. New York: Free Press, 1968.
Encyclopedia of Psychology. Eds. H. J. Eysenck and others. 3 vols. New York: Herder & Herder, 1972.
Harvard List of Books in Psychology. 4th ed. Cambridge, Mass.: Harvard Univ. Press, 1971.

International Encyclopedia of Psychiatry, Psychology, Psychoanalysis, and Neurology. New York: Van Nostrand Reinhold, 1977.

Loutitt, Chauncy M. *Handbook of Psychological Literature.* New York: Gordon, 1974.

Psychological Abstracts. Lancaster, Pa.: American Psychological Assn., 1927. (Monthly.)

Wilkening, Howard E. *The Psychology Almanac: A Handbook for Students.* Monterey, Calif.: Brooks-Cole, 1973.

Religion

Bach, Marcus. *Major Religions of the World: Their Origins, Basic Beliefs, and Development.* New York: Abingdon, 1977.

A Catholic Dictionary. Ed. Donald Attwater. New York: Macmillan, 1958.

Dictionary of American Religious Biography. Westport, Conn.: Greenwood Press, 1977.

Dictionary of Comparative Religion. Ed. S. G. F. Brandon. New York: Scribner's, 1970.

Encyclopaedia Judaica. 16 vols. New York: Macmillan, 1972.

Gaustad, Edwin S. *Historical Atlas of Religion in America.* Rev. ed. New York: Harper and Row, 1976.

Hastings, James. *Encyclopaedia of Religion and Ethics.* 2nd ed. 12 vols. New York: Scribner's, 1907–27.

Interpreter's Dictionary of the Bible. 4 vols. Nashville, Tenn.: Abingdon, 1962.

Kennedy, James R. *Library Research Guide to Religion and Theology.* Ann Arbor, Mich.: Pierian Press, 1974.

Mead, Frank S. *Handbook of Denominations in the United States.* 7th ed. Nashville, Tenn.: Abingdon, 1980.

Nelson's Complete Concordance of the New American Bible. Nashville, Tenn.: Nelson, 1977.

New Catholic Encyclopedia. 15 vols. New York: McGraw-Hill, 1967.

New Schaff-Herzog Encyclopedia of Religious Knowledge. 13 vols. Grand Rapids, Mich.: Baker Book House, 1949–50. (Two-volume supplement, *Twentieth Century Encyclopedia of Religions,* 1955.)

Oxford Dictionary of the Christian Church. Eds. F. L. Cross and Elizabeth A. Livingstone. 2nd ed. New York: Oxford Univ. Press, 1974.

A Reader's Guide to the Great Religions. Ed. Charles J. Adams. 2nd ed. New York: Free Press, 1977. (Bibliographical essays.)

Reese, William. *Dictionary of Philosophy and Religion, Eastern and Western.* Atlanta, Ga.: Humanics, 1978.

Religious and Theological Abstracts. Youngstown, Ohio: Theological Publishers, 1958—. (Quarterly.)

Rice, Edward. *Eastern Definitions: A Short Encyclopedia of Religions of the Orient.* Garden City, N.Y.: Doubleday, 1978.

Shorter Encyclopedia of Islam. Eds. H. A. Gibb and J. H. Kramers. Ithaca, N.Y.: Cornell Univ. Press, 1953.

Strong, James. *Exhaustive Concordance of the Bible.* London: Hodder & Stoughton, 1895. (Rpt. Nashville, Tenn.: Abingdon, 1963.)

Sociology

Abstracts for Social Workers. Albany, N.Y.: National Assn. of Social Workers, 1965—. (Quarterly.)

Bart, Pauline, and Linda Frankel. *The Student Sociologist's Handbook.* 3rd ed. Glenville, Ill.: Scott, Foresman, 1981.

Dictionary of Sociology and Related Sciences. Ed. Henry Pratt Fairchild. Totowa, N.J.: Littlefield, Adams, 1977.

Encyclopedia of Social Work. Ed. John Turner. New York: Assn. of Social Workers, 1965—. (Annually.)

Encyclopedia of Sociology. Ed. Gayle Johnson. Guilford, Conn.: Duskin, 1974.

The Harvard Encyclopedia of American Ethnic Groups. Ed. Stephan Thernstorm. Cambridge, Mass.: Harvard Univ. Press, 1980.

International Bibliography of Sociology. Chicago: Aldine, 1952—.(Annually.)

Mark, Charles. *Sociology of America: A Guide to Information Sources.* Detroit: Gale, 1976.

Sociological Abstracts. New York: Sociological Abstracts, 1952—. (Six issues a year.)

The Book of Women's Achievements. New York: Stein & Day, 1976.

Davis, Audrey B. *Bibliography on Women: With Special Emphasis on Their Roles in Science and Society.* New York: Science History, 1974.

Haber, Barbara. *Women in America: A Guide to Books, 1963–1975.* Boston: G. K. Hall, 1978.

Lerner, Gerda. *Black Women in White America.* New York: Pantheon, 1972.

Notable American Women, 1607–1950: A Biographical Dictionary. Eds. Edward T. James and others. 3 vols. Cambridge, Mass.: Harvard Univ. Press, 1971.

Notable American Women, the Modern Period: A Biographical Dictionary. Eds. Edward T. James and others. Cambridge, Mass.: Harvard Univ. Press, 1980.

Stineman, Esther. *Women's Studies: A Recommended Core Bibliography.* Littleton, Colo.: Libraries Unlimited, 1979.

Warren, Mary Anne. *The Nature of Women: An Encyclopedia and Guide to the Literature.* Inverness, Calif.: Edgepress, 1979.

Who's Who of American Women. Chicago: Marquis, 1958—. (Biennially.)

The Women's Rights Movement in the Seventies. Eds. Albert Krichmar and others. Metuchen, N.J.: Scarecrow Press, 1977.

The Women's Rights Movement in the United States, 1848–1970: A Bibliography and Sourcebook. Metuchen, N.J.: Scarecrow Press, 1972.

Women Studies Abstracts. Rush, N.Y.: Women's Studies, 1972—. (Quarterly. Annual index.)

Exercise C   Learning about the Library

In the spaces provided, answer the following questions about your college library.

1. What are the regular opening and closing hours on weekdays during the school year? _____
_____

2. Is the library open on Sundays? On holidays? _____

3. Who is the director or head librarian? _____
_____

4. For how long a period may books be withdrawn? _____
_____

5. What is the fine for overdue books? _____
_____

6. What system is used to classify books? _____
_____

7. Are catalog cards filed in one alphabetization (a dictionary catalog) or in separate author, title, and subject files (a divided catalog)? _____
_____

8. Which comes first in the card catalog:

   Capehart or Cape Kennedy? _____

   Newark or New York? _____

   Bay of Fundy or Bayard? _____

   In each case, note whether the alphabetization is done word-by-word or letter-by-letter.

9. Are the stacks open or closed? _____
_____

10. Where can you learn what periodicals the library has on file? _____
_____

11. Is there a browsing shelf? Where is it? _____
_____

12. Is there a record collection? Where is it? _____
_____

13. Is there a rare book room? Where is it? _____
_____

14. Where are the reserve shelves? _____
_____

15. Do undergraduates have Interlibrary Loan privileges? _____

16. Is there a duplicating or photocopying service? _____

17. Are study carrels available? _____

18. What microforms (microfilm, microcard, microprint, microfiche, ultrafiche) are available? _____
_____

19. Where are the readers for microfilm and microfiche? _____
_____

20. Are any computer services available? _____

21. Are clippings filed? Where is the file? _____
_____

Exercise D   Finding the Basic Library Tools

In a sketch of the library floor plan or by brief descriptions, locate each of the following:

1. Card catalog

2. *Readers' Guide*

3. Reserve books

4. Currrent magazines

5. Bound periodicals

6. Encyclopedias

7. *Union List of Serials*

8. *Who's Who in America*

9. Microfilm readers

10. *OED*

11. *Congressional Record*

12. Current fiction

Exercise E   Collecting Sources

Using either the card or computerized catalog, find two books related to the topic you are considering for your paper. Make a bibliography card for each. In *Readers' Guide* find two magazine articles related to your topic and make bibliography cards for them.

Exercise F   Selecting Reference Works

From the list of general reference works on pages 31–35, select the source most likely to supply information on each of the numbered items. Beneath each item write your first choice of a reference book and the information for any items assigned to you.

1. The Pulitzer Prize play in 1948

   Probable source: _____

   Information: _____

2. The father of Iphigenia

   Probable source: _____

   Information: _____

3. The symbol for the chemical element Strontium

   Probable source: _____

   Information: _____

4. The middle name of Walter Mondale

   Probable source: _____

   Information: _____

5. The origin of the word "radar"

   Probable source: _____

   Information: _____

6. The author of the line "Truth crushed to earth shall rise again"

   Probable source: _____

   Information: _____

7. The founder of the Behaviorist school of psychology

   Probable source: _____

   Information: _____

8. The title of a novel by Willa Cather

   Probable source: _____

   Information: _____

9. The composer of *Pictures at an Exhibition*

   Probable source: _____

   Information: _____

10. The chairman of the Senate Foreign Relations Committee

   Probable source: _____

   Information: _____

11. The world's record for women's discus throw

   Probable source: _____

   Information: _____

12. A magazine article on Panama published in 1984

   Probable source: _____

   Information: _____

13. The meaning of *glissando* in piano technique

   Probable source: _____

   Information: _____

14. The U.S. vice-president who served with Franklin Pierce

   Probable source: _____

   Information: _____

15. The major architectural achievement of Sir Christopher Wren

   Probable source: _____

   Information: _____

16. The birthplace of Robert Frost

   Probable source: _____

   Information: _____

17. The popular name for the belladonna plant

   Probable source: _____

   Information: _____

18. The latitude and longitude of Wake Island

   Probable source: _____

   Information: _____

19. The approximate size of the Kinorhyncha worm

   Probable source: _____

   Information: _____

20. The call number of *Nicholas Nickleby* by Charles Dickens

Probable source: _____

Information: _____

21. The geological term for the study of fossils

Probable source: _____

Information: _____

22. The title conferred on Benjamin Disraeli in 1876

Probable source: _____

Information: _____

23. The earliest meaning in English of the word "starve"

Probable source: _____

Information: _____

24. The historical event portrayed on the Bayeux tapestry

Probable source: _____

Information: _____

25. The date of the death of Senator Henry Jackson

Probable source: _____

Information: _____

THREE
GATHERING MATERIAL

A man cannot make fire but in proportion as he has fuel.

The ability to find books and periodicals in the library is a valuable skill, but it will not guarantee a successful research paper. You must also be able to discriminate among sources, select material relevant to your thesis, and take usable notes.

EVALUATING SOURCES

Perhaps because they rely so heavily on textbooks, some students have unwarranted reverence for whatever they see in print. Yet it is obvious that publication does not make a fact accurate or an opinion valid. Composing a research paper should improve your ability to evaluate material and judge the reliability of sources.

Criteria

Only a specialist can judge a source with finality. You may hesitate to accept or reject a source on the basis of your own knowledge, but the following points are significant when you must decide whether a source is trustworthy.

1. **Author.** An author's professional qualifications can usually be checked in a biographical reference book like *Who's Who in America.* Also, in scholarship, as in sports or entertainment, there are acknowledged stars, and as you investigate a particular subject, you soon come to recognize respected names.

2. **Title.** The full title of a book or an article usually indicates its content and purpose.
3. **Publisher.** As you work in a field, you will also learn the names of major publishers. Generally you can assume that their publications are trustworthy. In the same way, the reputation of a periodical may attest to the reliability of an article.
4. **Date.** The copyright year on the reverse of the title page will tell you how recent a book is. This is especially important with social or scientific subjects. An article on moon landings or women's liberation written before 1965 will probably not be very useful. An article on Shakespeare or the pyramids of Egypt, on the other hand, will not suffer so much from the passage of time.
5. **Preface.** Although many readers skip over introductory material almost as a reflex action, an author's preface may be a valuable preview of the content and purpose of the book.
6. **Table of contents.** The chapter titles indicate the major topics treated in a book.
7. **Illustrations.** Paging through a book will show you whether there are pictures, maps, diagrams, or other graphic materials that might be useful.
8. **Documentation.** An author's notes and bibliography are an indication, though not proof, of reliability. Furthermore, the bibliography may direct you to other treatments of the subject.
9. **Index.** The alphabetical listing of the topics covered in a book is not a sign of its reliability, but it can be very useful in determining its relevance. Students sometimes waste hours paging through books in search of information when a glance at the index would tell them whether their subject was discussed. In collecting material on the Salem witch trials, for example, you could check the indexes of twenty or more histories and biographies in less than an hour, looking for listings of "Judge Hathorne," "Salem," "witchcraft," and a few other related topics.
10. **Reviews.** It may be helpful to examine reviews of a book. Consult the volume of *Book Review Digest* covering the year when the book was published. Sometimes a review itself may prove to be a valuable source.
11. **Expert opinion.** For many subjects you could consult a faculty member or some other specialist regarding authorities in the field you are investigating.

Kinds of Sources

Besides judging the probable usefulness and reliability of a source, you should consider whether it is **primary** or **secondary**. The distinction is not as vital in an undergraduate paper as in advanced work, but it is significant.

Primary sources are firsthand materials like original documents, letters, or diaries. If, for example, you were writing about the drafting of the Constitution, the Constitution itself or a letter by one of the delegates would be a primary source. For a paper on *Nicholas Nickleby,* the novel itself would be a primary source.

Secondary sources are discussions of a subject after the fact. For example, a book by Charles A. Beard analyzing motives of the delegates to the Constitutional

Convention would be a secondary source. A biography of Charles Dickens and a history of the Yorkshire schools would also be secondary sources.

"Primary source" is an impressive term, but some primary sources, especially manuscripts when available, must be used with caution because they are often inaccurate or incomplete. A balanced mixture of primary and secondary materials, carefully chosen for their relevance to your thesis, may be desirable, but many student papers are based entirely on secondary sources.

Kinds of Material
(Exercise G)

Material that you find while reading will be of two general kinds: **fact** and **opinion.**

A fact states something that actually exists; it can be verified or proved. For example, the number of divorces in 1984, the amount of rainfall in 1983, or the date of the next election are verifiable facts. You use facts to support your ideas. A thesis statement cannot be totally factual, for it would not require development in an essay.

An opinion is an idea about a fact or about another opinion. It is an interpretation, a deduction, or a supposition. The reasons for a high number of divorces, the probable effect of rainfall on grain prices, and the outcome of the next election are opinions. Opinions taken from your sources can supply testimonial support but not absolute proof of your ideas. The crux of the thesis statement will be an opinion of your own.

Any research paper will include both facts and opinions taken from outside sources. The proportions will vary depending on the subject. It is important that you differentiate mentally between facts and opinions when you take notes from a source and when you incorporate them into your paper.

Supplementary Sources

Most of the supporting material for a research paper will come from books and periodicals, but you should not overlook other possibilities.

1. **Government publications.** (See p. 33.) The federal government is a prolific publisher of pamphlets and reports on all kinds of subjects. The Government Printing Office distributes more than one hundred million copies of various publications each year. Your major problem will be to discover what is available. After finding one or more titles, you have several options:

    a. Look for them in your own library or in nearby libraries. In each congressional district, there are two depository libraries entitled to receive copies of government bulletins.
    b. Order them from the Government Printing Office (Washington, D.C., 21401) or from the agency that issued them. Congressional committes are listed in the *Congressional Directory;* agencies of the executive branch are listed in the *United States Government Organization Manual.*

c. Write to your congressman asking for assistance.

Begin your search for such material as soon as possible. The process will probably take several weeks.

2. **Corporate publications.** Many companies publish pamphlets and brochures of various kinds in addition to their annual reports. A clear, courteous request will usually bring whatever materials are available. Such publications must be used with some caution because they are, after all, promotional in nature.

3. **Special collections.** The latest edition of *American Library Directory* (New York: Bowker, 1923—) will direct you to specialized collections. Since it is arranged geographically, you can easily check listings for nearby libraries as well as your own.

4. **Clippings.** Many libraries maintain a file of clippings, especially on subjects of local interest. Such files are often not listed in the card catalog and can be located only by asking a librarian.

5. **Reproductions.** In recent years many books, magazines, and newspapers have been reproduced on microforms. Because such reproductions are often listed in a separate file, you may overlook a wealth of material unless you consult a librarian.

6. **Interlibrary loans.** Sometimes a book or a copy of an article not available on your campus can be procured from another library. This service is not always open to undergraduates.

7. **Interviews.** A specialist in the field you are investigating can sometimes supply useful information. A paper on solar heating, for example, might be enhanced by a conversation with an architect or an engineer. But you should not invade the office of a total stranger without arranging an appointment in advance. Remember that your informant is undoubtedly busy. Devise pointed, thoughtful questions beforehand. Take notes as unobtrusively as possible and expand them as soon as possible after the interview. A tape recorder would be very useful if your informant approves. The interview should not be abused, but if conducted tactfully, it can be a valuable source of practical, firsthand information.

8. **Correspondence.** You should refrain from pestering busy specialists with letters requesting information that could be obtained from a reference book. You should also avoid vague requests for "all the information about" a subject. Sometimes, however, valuable data can be acquired by correspondence. Make your letter courteous, concise, and definite. A letter to a total stranger is usually not advisable. However, a friend of your family or an alumnus of your college may be considered fair game. If your topic involves another country, you might write to the United Nations delegation (see a Manhattan telephone directory) or to the embassy (see a Washington, D.C., directory). Address your letter to the Public Information Officer.

9. **Observation.** Some topics require and others permit that you visit a factory, a battlefield, an airport, or some other site. Decide in advance what you should look for. Take notes on the spot or as soon as possible after leaving.

Ingenuity and imagination in seeking material to supplement your library research will often improve a paper.

PURPOSIVE READING

Writing skill is essential in preparing a research paper, but your success will also depend on your ability to read carefully and take notes efficiently. By exploratory browsing through general sources, you choose a narrow topic. By analysis that is both thoughtful and imaginative, you decide on a tentative thesis and possible main points. You are then ready to begin collecting facts and opinions. Purposive reading is more selective than exploratory reading, and it requires the taking of notes.

Do not consider yourself fortunate if you find an entire book devoted to your topic; it may indicate that you are trying to cover too much in a short paper. Fairly brief passages in books and magazines are more likely to be useful. You can discover these relevant passages by checking the index of a book or by skimming a magazine article.

In using an article or a portion of a book, skim it first and then return to passages that look pertinent. It is difficult, if not impossible, to follow an author's train of thought if you interrupt your reading every few minutes to take notes. Devise a system for recording passages that look useful and then take notes after examining the source as a whole.

If you own the book or magazine, the simplest procedure is to star or underline a passage to which you expect to return. Do not underline a passage unless you are fairly certain of using it. The magic marker seems to have made underlining pleasurable for some students. They underline so much that they convert pages into variegated patterns of color that are barely readable. Any marking is unsuitable, of course, when you are using library sources.

Another procedure is to insert cards or slips of paper in the book as you read. After completing your reading, turn back to your starting point and make notes from the pages where you left bookmarks.

A third method is to keep track of usable passages on a piece of scratch paper. This is done most efficiently by using a decimal system for locating a passage on a page. For example, a sentence halfway down page 267 would be recorded as 267.5. A notation of content would also be useful. From a discussion of Valley Forge, for instance, you might record the following:

183.2   winter rations
183.7   fuel
184.6   description of von Steuben
188.4   types of drills

Always keep your thesis uppermost in your mind and use it to judge the relevance of material. If a fact or an opinion pertains to your thesis, it may belong in your paper. Take care to record it on a note card. If you doubt its pertinence, it is still prudent to record it because the book may be gone when you return to look for it later.

No matter how systematic and thorough your purposive reading and note-taking have been, you are almost certain after you start writing to discover gaps that must be filled. One reason for setting aside several days to write the paper is the likelihood of your needing to return to the library for additional research.

TAKING NOTES
(Exercise H)

A research paper cannot be written from memory. While doing the purposive reading, you collect facts and opinions that support your thesis. Collecting material for a research paper takes longer than the actual writing; therefore, purposive reading and note-taking should begin as early as possible. However, taking notes before you have narrowed your topic and formulated a thesis is risky; you may be tempted to keep the topic broad so that you can use all of your notes. With experience you will become more proficient in determining what notes to take and how to take them.

From the time you begin taking notes, you should realize that you are obligated to acknowledge the exact sources of all borrowed facts and opinions, whether or not you use the author's exact words. (See p. 103.) Of course, facts that are common knowledge are not cited. You would not credit a source with the information that the Battle of Hastings was fought in 1066 or that Shakespeare was born in Stratford. Usually your sense of obligation to a source will be clear-cut. Occasionally you will be confronted with an ethical question: "Is this information attributable to only one source, is it general knowledge, or is it the product of your own thinking?" An honest intention to give credit for borrowed material and understanding of the forms and uses of notes (see pp. 123–24) will ensure adequate documentation and avoid any suggestion of plagiarism. (See pp. 103–04.)

Three brief examples based on the passage on page 63 illustrate uses and misuses of borrowed material.

Dashiel Hamett developed the Continental Op for <u>Black Mask</u> in 1929

and later used him in a novel, <u>Red Harvest</u>. The Op is a professional

who does well what he is paid to do.

The above passage is flagrant plagiarism. There is no reference number to a note that would acknowledge the source. The student has not only borrowed the content but garbled it; Hammett's name is misspelled, and the first sentence of the source has been misinterpreted. Language from the source has not been enclosed in quotation marks.

Dashiel Hammett's Continental Op is a complicated character, forty

years old, rather fat, and very tough. Emotions divert the attention

and impair efficiency, so he avoids them.[1]

This example has a reference number, which suggests that the source is identified in a note, but otherwise it is almost as reprehensible as the first example. The student has simply made a loose paraphrase of the source, changing some words but using some of the original phrasing without quotation marks. This kind of haphazard paraphrase is probably the most common form of plagiarism.

Dashiel Hammett's Continental Op, according to Russel Nye, "is a professional, doing well what he is paid to do . . . scrupulously honest, not because of any ethical commitments but because his job demands it."[1]

This example illustrates legitimate use of borrowed material. The phrase "according to Russel Nye" identifies the source. It is not strictly necessary because this information will be in the note. Quotation marks are used accurately, and the ellipsis indicates an omission of words from the original.

So that citations will be accurate in your paper, you will need the source, including the page number, on every note card. Write this information at the top of the card before making your note. While you are working in the library, either scholarly zeal or careless haste may cause you to take notes rapidly; after filling one card, you immediately begin another. It is fatally easy, therefore, to forget to record the source and the page number at the bottom of the card. There are few activities so depressing as searching through a five-hundred-page volume to locate a passage that you neglected to record.

When you first decide to use a source, make out a bibliography card (see pp. 7–8) that includes the author's name, the title, and the publication data. Since you have this card for reference, you need only a code word (usually the author's last name) and the page number on each note card. Another method is to assign each bibliography card a Roman numeral or a capital letter and write this symbol and the page number on each card. Using the author's name is less confusing. At any rate, copying the complete title of a source on every card is a waste of time.

It is also helpful to label each note card in the upper right-hand corner with a brief phrase (sometimes called a "slug") indicating its content. If your outline has taken shape, you can use the appropriate outline symbol. When you are ready to write your rough draft, you can glance at each label and sort the cards into related groups. Otherwise, you would need to read each card through to decide where it belonged. To some extent, the habit of labeling your notes will make you a more selective note-taker because it will compel you to consider the function of each note and to keep your thesis and outline clearly in mind.

After summarizing material from a source, compare the notes that you have taken with the original to be certain that you have not inadvertently echoed key phrases that should be in quotation marks.

A quotation must be copied exactly as it appears in the original source. After copying a quotation, compare your version with the printed text to ensure that you have copied it accurately. Doing this habitually will prevent transcription errors, which are fatally easy to make. Should there be an error in the source, insert *sic* (thus) after it in brackets. Do not use *sic* after a British spelling like "colour" or "centre" or after an alternative spelling like "judgement." Students are sometimes eager to use *sic,* but the occasion seldom arises. You should, however, know what the word means when you encounter it in your reading. Do not use it sarcastically to indicate disagreement or disapproval, and do not follow it with an exclamation point.

Although you cannot change a quoted passage, you can omit words from it. As long as you do not distort the meaning, you can omit a phrase or even several sentences. The omission is indicated by an ellipsis (. . .), three spaced periods, which is a legitimate, though often misused, punctuation mark. To facilitate blending a short quotation into your own sentence, you may omit the ellipsis at the beginning or at the close if the meaning of the passage is not altered in any way. An ellipsis is always needed, of course, when words are deleted within the quotation. It is even possible to combine quotations from two different paragraphs. In this case, a line of periods across the page indicates the point where sentences have been deleted. Such extensive elision is seldom found in student papers. It is dangerously easy to distort the original context, and, in addition, students are not encouraged to quote such long passages.

Frequently, judicious pruning of a quotation will enable you to blend it more smoothly into the text of your essay. (See pp. 173–75.) Also, a word or a brief phrase within brackets may clarify a passage so that less of the original must be quoted.

"Emerson was convinced that he [Thoreau] had wasted his time on trivialities."

"The uncertainty of his employment [at MGM] increased Fitzerald's anxieties about his finances and about his future."

If your typewriter is not equipped with a key for square brackets, draw them in as neatly as possible. Hand-drawn brackets [ ] are preferable to those made with the typewriter slash and the underline: /⎺ ⎺7.

Kinds of Notes

The notes that you will take will be direct quotations, various forms of summary, and combinations of quotation and summary.

Although students' papers are often overloaded with quotations, this cannot be said of their note cards. If you are in doubt about whether you will use an author's actual words, take down the quotation. When you write the first draft, you can convert a quotation into a summary, but you cannot substitute a quotation for a summary without returning to the original source. There are four general reasons for using a direct quotation:

1. **Accuracy:** when the precise language of the original is crucial.
2. **Authority:** when the exact words of a source carry more weight than a summary.
3. **Conciseness:** when a quotation states an idea in fewer words than a summary could do.
4. **Vividness:** when the language is more colorful or more descriptive than your summary would be.

If you cannot justify a quotation by one or more of these reasons, you probably should summarize a passage in your own words. A citation will still be necessary.

Remember to write the author's last name and the page number in the upper left-hand corner along with a word or two indicating the content in the upper right-hand corner. Various kinds of note cards are illustrated below by samples based on the following passage from *The Unembarrassed Muse* by Russel Nye. (Pagination of the source is cited in parentheses.)

> Dashiell Hammett began to develop the character of his private detective, the Continental Op, for *Black Mask* and in 1929 wrote him into a novel, *Red Harvest*, serialized in the magazine. The Op, a more complicated character than most of his companions, fortyish, a bit fat, and very tough—appeared again the same year in *The Dain Curse*, but in *The Maltese Falcon* (1930) Sam Spade replaced him. The investigator of *The Glass Key* (1931) was not a detective but Ned Beaumont, a racketeer's bodyguard. A study of character and brutality, it remains the most complex of Hammett's novels. *The Thin Man* (1934) shifted to Nick Charles, an exdetective who wanted only to be left alone to enjoy his bourbon and his pretty wife but who got involved in murder over his protest. The heart of Hammett's work lies in his first four novels, his three Sam Spade stories, and his early Continental Op series.
>
> The Op, Spade, and Beaumont—Hammett's three versions of the tough hero—have similarities and differences. The Op is a professional, doing well what he is paid to do. He is scrupulously honest, not because of any ethical commitments but because his job demands it. He cleans up a corrupt city in *Red Harvest* because a man hired him to do it; that it will be just as corrupt five years hence matters not at all. "Emotions are nuisances during business hours," so he has none. Sex, hate, and anger divert the attention and impair efficiency; there is, he says, "hard skin over what's left of my soul . . . after twenty years of messing around with crime." His closest approach to introspection occurs in *Red Harvest*, when after causing sixteen deaths in a week he wonders briefly if he likes killing too much—"Play with murder enough, and it gets you one of two ways; it makes you sick or you get to like it . . . . "   *(259)*
>
> Spade, described by Hammett as "a hard, shifty fellow, always able to take care of himself, able to get the best of anybody," is a more reflective man. A professional like The Op, Spade nevertheless has a large area of ambiguous gray in his character. Neither he nor the reader is sure he will deny himself the woman, reject the bribe, or find no pleasure in killing, nor does it really matter to him. Through Spade, Hammett came closer than anywhere else to a philosophical position—since life is disorderly and confused one cannot plan for it; one can only adjust to it, and in the end it is probably enough to have taken care of yourself.
>
> Yet Spade does have an elementary if somewhat bruised belief in something positive. In his list of seven reasons for turning his bedmate Brigid O'Shaughnessy over to the police at the end of *The Maltese Falcon*, he cites first the fact that she had killed his partner—a man he hated, but still his partner.   *(260)*

Before taking any notes from a source, make a bibliography card like the one below. If you postpone making the card until you have finished taking notes, you may forget to make it and have to return to the library and locate the source. It will save trouble if you write the bibliographical information as it will appear in your final bibliography.

Nye, Russell. *The Unembarrassed Muse: The Popular Arts in America*. New York: Dial Press, 1970.

E. 169.1

N92

Bibliography card for The Unembarrassed Muse

Four kinds of note cards are illustrated below:

1. **Quotation note.** A quotation must be copied exactly as it appears in the source and must be enclosed in quotation marks. The sample note below omits seven words from the second sentence. The omission is indicated by an ellipsis (. . .).

Nye, p. 260   Spade's code

"Spade does have an elementary if somewhat bruised belief in something positive.
In his list of seven reasons for turning his bed mate Brigid O'Shaughnessy over to the police. . . , he cites first the fact that she had killed his partner-- a man he hated, but still his partner."

Quotation note

2. **Summary note.** A summary in complete sentences is probably the least practical form of note. If the author's language is not used and only the content is significant, an outline note might be sufficient. The summary should not echo the style of the source. The example below sums up one aspect of Hammett's detectives as they are described in the selection.

Nye, pp. 259-60   cynicism

Hammett's detectives have no idealistic motives for solving crimes. After a crime is solved, there is no suggestion that human nature or society will be improved.

Summary note

3. **Outline note.** If only factual information is taken from a source, rough notes in outline form may be sufficient. Abbreviations and other shortcuts that could not be used in a quotation note are permissible here. A danger in this type of note-taking is that if overused, it may encourage you to follow one source too closely. The example below tabulates facts from the first paragraph.

Nye, p. 259   H's dets.

Continental Op – <u>Red Harvest</u> 1929

             & <u>Dain Curse</u> 1929

Sam Spade – <u>The Maltese Falcon</u> 1930

Ned Beaumont – <u>The Glass Key</u> 1931

      (a gangster's bodyguard)

Nick Charles – <u>The Thin Man</u> 1934

      (a former det.)

Outline note

4. **Combination note.** A note may combine quotation and summary. For the experienced writer of research papers, this type of note is the most useful because it encourages the blending of quoted material with the writer's sentences. In a way, when you write a combination note, you are beginning to compose your essay. It is especially important to be meticulous in the use of quotation marks. The page numbers within the note are an optional safeguard; when a note contains material from more than one page, it is prudent to label it in this way so that your citation will be accurate if you use only part of the note in your paper.

> Nye, pp. 259-60   loyaties
>
> Hammett's detectives have few commitments.
> The Continental Op "is a professional,
> doing well what he is paid to do." (259)
> Sam Spade "has a large area of ambiguous
> gray in his character." His only loyalty
> is to his dead partner. (260)

Combination note

Note Cards

Like most professional scholars, students generally find that material can be recorded most efficiently on cards. Each card should contain material relating to the same point. Ordinarily all material on a card will be taken from the same source, but sometimes brief notes from two different sources can be written on the same card if they are closely related and are certain to be used together in the paper. Be certain that each source is clearly identified.

The reason for using cards is that they can be manipulated and rearranged as often as necessary. Notes taken in a notebook are frozen in a single order and are difficult to organize. You may find yourself following one source too closely or overlooking important points. In desperation, many students have taken shears and clipped notebook pages into slips so that they could arrange them in sequence. The height, or depth, of inefficiency is to take notes in a bound notebook and write on both sides of the page. Even shears are of no avail in this dilemma, except for *hara-kiri.*

By experimenting, you can find what type of card is best suited to your writing habits. Memo pads are satisfactory in size and are inexpensive, but the pages tend to stick together. A 3 × 5 card is too small for some notes; the 5 × 8 card invites the writing of too much material on a card. The 4 × 6 card, therefore, is a happy medium. Most of your notes will not be long enough to fill more than one side, but there is no really good reason for not writing on both sides of a card if necessary. When you spread a note over two cards, you run the risk of losing or misplacing one of them. To make certain that you do not overlook the reverse side, write "OVER" at the bottom of the card. Since penciled notes tend to smudge, it is advisable to take notes in ink or on a typewriter.

Note Sheets

Despite unanimous advocacy of note cards in manuals like this one, some students resist using them. If note cards are not required by your instructor and if you have a strong aversion to using them, you can take notes on sheets of paper. A legal-size pad is most suitable. Do not take all the notes from a source on the same sheet because you are almost certain to overlook some items when you start to write. Take notes topically; write all notes pertaining to the same topic on the same sheet. Space them generously so that you can use arrows, numbers, and other annotations to indicate where or how they will be used in the paper. (See p. 70.) Note cards are strongly recommended, but if you follow some other method make certain that it is efficient.

Photocopies

The widespread availability of copying machines has revolutionized note-taking techniques for some students and professional scholars. After selecting passages that you plan to use, you can take your books and journals and a roll of dimes to a photocopier and in a few minutes duplicate each page. Before leaving the library, write the source at the top of each copy and be certain that each page has been reproduced legibly. The major advantages of photocopying are that you reduce the possibility of transcription errors and, perhaps, that after making the copies you can work in more relaxed surroundings. A disadvantage, besides the expense, is that you may find the photocopied pages unwieldy and difficult to manage. Essentially, after you have copied forty pages and taken them to your room, you have just what you had in the library—forty pages of print. You still must decide what to quote, what to summarize, and what to omit. Cards are still useful. It may be advisable to write summary notes on cards and to clip out passages that you expect to quote and tape or paste them on cards. Do not neglect the reference at the top of each card. Taking notes by using photocopies is not always as efficient as it appears, and it may be wise to adopt it gradually as you aquire greater skill in evaluating material and in composing a research paper.

Allen Eyles, <u>The</u> <u>Western</u>   FILMS

pp. 48-49
omit
    <u>They</u> <u>Died</u> "whitewashes" C.
    lists 22 actors who have played C.

Utley (<u>They</u> <u>Died</u>)

p. 119
?
    "Errol Flynn stands 'like a sheaf of corn,
    with all ears fallen around him,' waiting
    for the Sioux lance that will end his
    life and a three-hour motion picture."

Fenin (<u>They</u> <u>Died</u>)

p. 11
omit
    "a clear-cut example of historical incident
    being manipulated to suit script
    requirements"

Fenin (<u>LBM</u>)

p. 370

use part
    "Penn uses the film to express his personal
    philosophy with vigor, saving his most
    passionate feeling for describing past horrors
    reminiscent of present ones. His excoriation
    of George Armstrong Custer is one of the most
    pitiless indictments of a pompous fool
    ever witnessed on the screen."

Exercise G   Differentiating Fact and Opinion

Classify the statments below as Fact (F), Opinion (O), or a combination of both (FO). If a statement contains both fact and opinion, underline factual portions and enclose opinions in parentheses.

_____   1. Henry James was born in New York City on 15 April 1843.

_____   2. His father was a student of philosophy and theology.

_____   3. As a young man he studied painting, and he often seems to compose a scene with a painter's eye.

_____   4. Because James felt an unconscious rivalry with his brother, William, he sometimes portrayed elder brothers in his novels as unpleasant characters.

_____   5. *Daisy Miller,* first published in 1878, portrays an innocent young girl destroyed by her own inexperience and by the cruelty of expatriate Americans.

_____   6. James's mother died in January, 1882, and his father died in December of the same year.

_____   7. *The Bostonians* is his only full-length novel with an American setting.

_____   8. James is sometimes described as a "novelist's novelist" because of his devotion to his craft and his concern with technique.

_____   9. In 1897 he moved to Lamb House in Sussex, where he spent the remainder of his life, happily taking part in the simple village life.

_____   10. His greatest novel, *The Ambassadors,* was published in 1903.

_____   11. Between 1905 and 1908 he revised many of his works for the "New York Edition," improving the style and strengthening characterization.

_____   12. In 1904 he returned to America for the first time in twenty years, and his book about this experience, *The American Scene,* suggests that he viewed the rapid pace of American life with bewildered disapproval.

_____   13. In June, 1915, he became a British citizen.

_____   14. In 1920 a useful selection of his letters was edited by Percy Lubbock.

Exercise H   Taking Notes

The selection below is reprinted from *The Comic Mind: Comedy and the Movies,* 2nd ed., by Gerald Mast. It was published in 1979 by Univ. of Chicago Press. The paragraphs are numbered and the page numbers of the original are cited within parentheses for use in the exercises that follow.

1   The Marx Brothers and W. C. Fields were the legitimate descendants of the American iconoclastic tradition. Like John Bunny, Mack Sennett, Chaplin, and Keaton, these comics made films that ridiculed the sweet, the nice, the polite, the acceptable. Significantly, their films ridiculed other films as well as social customs. As the silent filmmakers had earlier discovered, to parody "serious" films was also to parody the values on which those films (and society as a whole) were built. Although more famed as masters of comic performance, the Marx Brothers and W. C. Fields performed in films with very personal and individual conceptions. Lacking complete control over their material (and, later in their careers, not even interested in such control), the Marx Brothers were dependent on their writers. And at Paramount those writers gave them very surprising, iconoclastic things to do. The Marx Brothers films were far closer in both spirit and method to the dialogue comedies than to the later funnyman sound films. Fields, on the other hand, gained complete control over the writing of his own films at Universal. And their deliberate sloppiness was Fields' own kind of statement about the pretentious gentility of the well-made film.

2   The Marx Brothers' three best films at Paramount—*Monkey Business* (1931), *Horsefeathers* (1932), and *Duck Soup* (1933)—all hurl comic mud at the gleaming marble pillars of the American temple. The target of *Monkey Business* is money and high society; the rich society snobs merely happen to be gangsters who made their money from bootlegging. The target of *Horsefeathers* is the university; knowledge and the pursuit of it are reduced to thievery, bribery, lechery, and foolishness. The target of *Duck Soup* is democracy and government itself; grandiose political ceremonies, governmental bodies, international diplomacy, the law courts, and war are reduced to the absurd. All three films also parody popular "serious" genres—gangster films, college films, and romantic-European-kingdom films. The implication of this spoofing is that the sanctified institution is as hollow and dead as the cinematic cliché; the breezy, chaotic, revolutionary activities of the comic anarchists give society's respectable calcifications a much-deserved comeuppance.   *(281)*

3   The Marx Brothers could get away with subversion because of their sheer madness. The brothers, like Ben Turpin in the silents, were pure loons, creatures from some other world, and this distance from reality gave them powerful privileges. To sustain a full-length film (the parodic silents with loons like Turpin and Snub Pollard were purposely shorts), the Marx Brothers' pictures capitalized on diversity. Each of the brothers had his distinct comic style—Groucho's brazenly nasty double-talk, Chico's artfully stupid malapropisms, Harpo's startling physical horseplay. Zeppo added a fourth dimension in the Paramounts as the cliché of the straight man and juvenile, the bland, wooden espouser of sentiments that seem to exist only in the world of the sound stage. The Marx Brothers' Paramounts

added up these four kinds of human comedy—plus musical numbers (some parodic, some not), plus the central parodic idea of the films, plus the individual pieces of intellectual and visual parody. They overcame the sound film's limitations on the single comic performer through multiplicity and addition rather than unity.

4   The Marx Brothers also overcame the problem of the talkies by revealing individual relationships to talk. Groucho talks so much, so rapidly, and so belligerently that talk becomes a kind of weapon. He shoots word bullets at his listeners, rendering them (and the audience) helpless, gasping for breath, trying to grab hold of some argument long enough to make sense of it. But before anyone can grab a verbal handle, Groucho has already moved on to some other topic and implication that seems to follow from his previous one—but doesn't. Groucho's ceaseless talk leads the listener in intellectual circles, swallowing us in a verbal maze, eventually depositing us back at the starting point without knowing where we have been or how we got there. Groucho's "logic" is really the manipulation of pun, homonym, and equivocation. He substitutes the quantity of sound and the illusion of rational connection for the theoretical purpose of talk—logical communication.

5   Chico's relationship to talk also substitutes sound for sense and the appearance of meaning for meaning. To Chico, "viaduct" sounds like "why a duck," "wire fence" like "why a fence," "shortcut" like "short cake," "sanity clause" like "Santa Claus," "dollars" like "Dallas," "taxes" like "Texas." He alone can puncture Groucho's verbal spirals by stopping the speeding train of words and forcing Groucho to respond to his own erroneous intrusions. Groucho cannot get away with his coy substitution of sound for sense when Chico makes different (but similar) sounds out of the key terms in Groucho's verbal web. Chico's absurd accent (this Italian burlesque would be considered very impolite by later standards) makes him hear Groucho's words as if he, the Italian who speaks pidgin English, were speaking them. *(282)*

6   The substitution of sound for sense reaches its perfection in Harpo, who makes only sounds. Harpo substitutes whistling and beeps on his horn for talk. Ironically, he communicates in the films as well as anybody. He communicates especially well with Chico, who understands Harpo better than Groucho does. Chico continually interprets Harpo's noises for Groucho. The irony that a bumbling foreign speaker renders a mute clown's honks, beeps, and whistles into English so it can be understood by the supreme verbal gymnast plays a role in every Marx Brothers film.

7   Harpo also substitutes the language of the body for speech. In this system of communication, Harpo uses two powerful allies—props and mime. He gives the password ("swordfish") that admits him to a speakeasy by pulling a swordfish out of his pocket. He impersonates Maurice Chevalier by miming a Chevalier song to a phonograph record, produced out of his coat especially for the occasion. Or he orders a shot of Scotch in the speakeasy by snapping into a Highland fling. In these early talkies, talk became one of the comic subjects of the films as well as one of the primary comic devices. As in the early Chaplin sound films, Marx Brothers made talk an ally simply by treating it so specially. *(283)*

Make the note cards described below.

1. Make a bibliography card for the Mast book, using the information in the heading on page 73.
2. Write as a quotation note the first two sentences of Paragraph 1. Omit the first

ten words of the second sentence and substitute the word "They."

3. Write a summary note condensing Paragraph 2 in your own words. Do not try to include all the substance of the original.

4. Write an outline note based on Paragraphs 4, 5, 6, and 7. Be certain that all of your notes pertain to one idea.

5. Write as a quotation note the first two sentences of Paragraph 6. Omit the last three words of the first sentence and the first word of the second.

6. Write a combination note based on Paragraph 3, combining at least two phrases from the original with one or more sentences of your own.

FOUR
CONSTRUCTING AN OUTLINE

A plan formed by mature consideration and diligent selection out of all the schemes which may be offered.

Just as some persons insist that they cannot learn to spell, multiply decimals, or operate a manual gearshift, some students doggedly maintain that they are unable to construct an outline before writing a paper. They may be unwilling to exert the mental effort required, they may feel that a predetermined plan will inhibit their creativity, or they may be genuinely convinced that an outline serves no useful purpose. In fact, however, the procedure involved in outlining is basic in successful written or oral communication: formulation of a tentative thesis or central idea, division of the thesis into main points, organization of supporting material for each main point. Outlining is not just the construction of a diagram; it is a mode of thinking. It is not a separate step in the writing of a research paper; it begins with the choice of a topic and is involved in every subsequent step. Sometimes a student who is averse to outlining will prepare an outline after writing a paper, an activity as futile as charting the route after completing a trip.

An outline, in the broadest sense, is a summarizing list. It reduces a collection of material to its essential parts. Outlines are of two general kinds: the **running outline,** which is a listing of details and ideas in no particular order, and the **formal outline,** which shows the order, the relationships, and the relative importance of its parts.

A formal outline may be composed of words and phrases (topics) or of sentences. The same basic process is followed in constructing topic and sentence outlines. Each type has its advantages. The sentence outline is more complete, but it often seems verbose. The topic outline, which reduces every item to a noun or a noun phrase, is more concise but often seems uninformative. The advantages of each type can be achieved in a combination outline, in which main points are sentences and subpoints are topics. Writing a sentence for each paragraph or larger unit of a paper helps assure that each will be unified by a clear-cut purpose. Topics are sufficient to identify steps in the development. (For examples of all three types of formal outlines, see pp. 87–90.)

USES OF OUTLINES

You may use outlines in many different ways. The type of outline you need will depend on the purpose for which it is intended.

Class Notes

Class notes should be kept in outline form. You will find, perhaps through bitter experience, that without some record of class lectures review is impossible. A running outline is worthless for review; after a few weeks it is impossible to recall the interrelationships of ideas. A formal outline will preserve both the pattern and the substance of a lecture. Since class notes are solely for your own use, you should develop your private system of abbreviations and other shortcuts. You may prefer to omit outline symbols and use only indentation to show subordination of ideas. At any rate, notes resembling a formal outline are much more functional than a series of phrases separated by dashes. Classroom lectures are usually an elaboration of two to five main ideas. Listen for major points and their subdivisions. Transitional signals like "Second," "Next," or "On the other hand" will help you identify the divisions of thought.

Class Assignments

An outline of a chapter in a book or an article in a periodical may be an assignment to be handed in or it may be the best method of mastering the material. First, skim the pages to be outlined, searching for the author's main idea and its chief subdivisions. Then reread the material carefully, looking for supporting subtopics. If you prepare such an outline as an assignment, you should observe the conventions of a formal outline.

Running Outline

The running outline serves only as a kind of mental inventory. You simply jot down facts and ideas that relate to your subject. A private brain-storming session in which you free associate can be a productive procedure if followed by judicious evaluation of the material. There is no special order in a running outline except the random order in which facts and ideas come into your mind. Before they are sorted and organized, notes for a research paper are an extensive running outline.

Working Outline

The working outline for a paper should use the symbols and other conventions of a formal outline (see pp. 80–81). It is a tentative prospectus evolved in the early stages of a writing project and may range in extent from three or four phrases jotted in an examination booklet to a detailed plan for a twenty-page paper. Whatever its length, it should be kept flexible. An outline is a tool, not a fetter. A good outline evolves; it is not composed in a single operation. The student who makes an outline and then adheres to it blindly may work under a handicap almost as great as the student who tries to write without making a preliminary plan. A working outline is tentative until the paper is completed. Your revisions will be of three general kinds:

1. You will add some topics, and you will delete others.
2. You will reevaluate topics. What originally seemed worth a main topic may be worth only a subtopic. A subtopic, on the other hand, may expand into a main point.
3. You will rearrange the order of the topics and subtopics to facilitate transitions and improve coherence in the essay.

A working outline can be constructed from a running outline, which is your stockpile of material. As you look over a rough list of items, you use your imagination and your common sense to discover relationships. You look for groupings that are logical and consistent, testing and discarding a half-dozen patterns before finding the one best suited to your purpose. As in any construction, you must reconcile yourself to some waste; a running outline is certain to contain items that will not fit into your essay. Papers sometimes lack unity because students try to squeeze into them every fact and opinion found in their exploratory reading.

Final Outline

The final outline is intended for the reader. It should, therefore, be in a logical form and should observe accepted outlining conventions.

If an outline is to be handed in with your research paper, you should revise your working outline as you write. Structural improvements may occur to you as you write the final draft of the paper, and so it might be wise to postpone the final draft of the outline until the paper has been completed. This suggestion is not a justification for neglecting to make a thoughtful working outline.

The final outline should be an accurate diagram of the design of a paper. It is a bird's-eye view of the organization. Because it includes only the steps in the development, it will be less detailed than the working outline. It resembles the blueprint for a house; the blueprint shows the location of a wall, but it does not show the number of nails it contains or the color it will be painted.

CONVENTIONS OF OUTLINING

The purpose of a formal outline is to show graphically the order, the unity, and the relative importance of the various parts of an essay. To show these qualities, certain conventional devices are in general use.

1. Values are shown by symbols. The most common system is very simple:

    I.

    II.

        A.

        B.

            1.
            2.

                a.
                b.

    To subdivide further, you merely alternate Arabic numerals and lowercase letters. But if you subdivide to that extent, you are probably including too many details or you have omitted a necessary main heading. You will seldom deal with a set of ideas on five or six levels of importance. Symbols are an important way of showing relative values because all items with the same kind of symbol are of approximately the same importance. Something is wrong with an outline in which A represents a paragraph and B represents a single sentence. Items below the second rank (capital letters) are usually single-spaced.

2. Indentation is another means of showing values. All headings on the same margin are assumed to be of approximately the same importance. Note that Roman numerals are aligned on the right:

    I.

    II.

3. Parallelism, also a means of showing values, means in an outline just what it means in connected prose: ideas of equal importance are given equal or like expression. In a topic outline every item should be a word or a phrase; in a sentence outline every item should be a sentence. It is not necessary, however, that every item contain the same number of words; headings are parallel when they are in the same grammatical form. For a simple example of parallelism, turn back to the Table of Contents and compare the chapter headings, which are all gerunds: Choosing, Using, Gathering, Constructing, Documenting, Writing.

4. In a topic outline every heading should be a noun or the equivalent of a noun (a gerund or, possibly, an infinitive). Most nonparallel items can easily be converted to nouns, and the revised form is usually more concise:

Virile = Virility
In Upper Michigan every summer = Summers in Upper Michigan
Lived in Cuba = Residence in Cuba
Married four times = Four marriages
As a boy he loved hunting and fishing = Boyhood love of hunting and fishing

5. The extent to which topics are subdivided should be consistent. Ordinarily for a research paper the subdivisions of each paragraph are represented in the outline. In most outlines you will be tempted at least once to list minor details simply because they are so obvious. If one Roman numeral is merely broken into two subtopics and the next Roman numeral is subdivided as far as lowercase letters, the outline is probably faulty.

6. Single division is a logical error in either type of formal outline. A single symbol, therefore, is a danger signal. When you indent and begin a set of subordinate symbols, you are dividing ideas. Since nothing can divide into only one part, you must have at least two subtopics or none at all.

7. Avoid if possible the use of general terms like "Introduction," "Conclusion," "Example," or "Summary." A heading should signify the content of a portion of an essay, not its purpose or method.

8. To conform to the last two conventions (no single divisions and no omnibus headings), write the thesis at the top of the outline page and then begin the outline proper. If the central idea of an essay is included in the outline as I, no other idea can rank with it, and adding a II with some vague heading like *Development* or *Body* would merely complicate the outline. Writing the thesis separately is also a valuable test of your mastery of your topic; if you cannot formulate a thesis sentence, you probably need to narrow your topic further or reconsider your objective. The conclusion that will appear in the paper should not be included in the outline since it will be substantially the same as the thesis.

THE OUTLINING PROCESS

When you construct an outline, your major tasks are **classification** and **arrangement**—dividing facts and opinions into categories and arranging the divisions in a logical order.

Classification
(Exercises I and J)

The basic procedure in the outlining process is classification, which means sorting ideas and facts into categories. Examples of classification can be seen on every hand. In all aspects of our lives, we take for granted the more or less orderly division of ideas and things into functional groupings: classified ads in a newspaper, the Seven Deadly Sins, the yellow pages in a telephone directory, the sections in a symphony orchestra, the colleges in a university and the departments in a college, offensive and defensive units on a football team, the parts of speech, genera and species in biology, the three branches of the national government, the signs of the zodiac, and zones in a city plan.

Classification can proceed in two directions—from general to specific (deductive) or from specific to general (inductive). For example:

1. **General to specific.** For a paper on recreation, you might decide in advance to divide your material on the basis of the kinds of sites that are used (courts, fields, parks, and playgrounds) and then look for activities conducted on each type of site.

2. **Specific to general.** You might list twenty or more recreational activities in a running outline and then group them on some logical basis. You could classify them on the basis of the kinds of sites used, age groups, their means of support, the degree of participation, the seasons of the year, or any other basis appropriate to your thesis.

Actually, in constructing an outline you use both types of classification. When you look over a running outline in search of categories, you are working from specific to general. When you decide that you need a certain topic in an outline and then look for material to support it, you are working from general to specific. In analyzing a completed outline, follow a deductive approach: consider first the thesis, then the main headings, and finally each set of subheadings.

To classify any collection of miscellaneous material for an outline or for any purpose, you need a guiding principle to serve as a means of determining whether an item belongs and where it belongs. This principle is called the **basis of division.** Words are classified into parts of speech on the basis of function; boxers are classified in divisions on the basis of weight; history is divided into periods on the basis of time; library books are classified on the basis of their subject matter; engines are classified on the basis of horsepower; the United States is divided into time zones, area codes, and postal zones on the basis of space.

Consider some possible bases for classifying a group of three hundred college students:

1. Childhood diseases
2. Credits completed
3. Physical condition
4. Parents' income
5. Sex
6. Automobile ownership

The first classification might be useful to the student health service, the second to the registrar, the third to the athletic department, the fourth to the alumni office, the fifth to sororities and fraternities, and the sixth to the campus police. But classification on the basis of childhood diseases would be of no value to the campus police, and a classification that divided half the students on the basis of physical condition and the other half on the basis of sex would be of no value to anyone. The basis of division in any classification should be functional, and it should be followed consistently.

The basis of division should be consistent in each section of an outline, but variety is also important. First, find a logical basis for dividing your material into main points and adhere to it. Then subdivide each of the main points. If you subdivide one main topic on a chronological basis, try to subdivide the next one on the basis of space or some abstract consideration like cause and effect or reasons pro and con. A paper in which every main point is subdivided in the same way will inevitably be monotonous.

To ensure logical classification, keep in mind three principles:

1. In any series of headings of like rank, do not shift the basis of division. Such inconsistency is probably the most common violation of outlining logic. The following main headings for a paper on local color fiction are an extreme example:

   I.   The South

   II. Short stories

   III. 1865-75

   IV. Bret Harte

   V.   The Atlantic Monthly

   VI. Reasons for popularity

   This paper could probably be organized most effectively on the basis of geographical regions (I); but it could also be planned from the standpoint of literary forms (II), chronology (III), individual writers (IV), modes of publication (V), or logical analysis (VI). But unless one of these bases was adhered to throughout, the divisions would be certain to overlap. The six main headings above could not possibly produce a coherent essay.

2. Categories should be mutually exclusive so that they do not overlap. A plan in which a subtopic might fit under two or three different main topics would be confusing to a reader—and to the writer. Actually, if a consistent basis of division is observed in each set of headings, mutual exclusiveness will result. In the example above, Bret Harte could be discussed under any of the main headings except the first because he published popular short stories in *The Atlantic Monthly* in the early 1870's. But he could be treated only in II if the basis of division was spatial or geographical:

   I.   The South

   II. The Far West

   III. New England

   IV. The Midwest

3. The subdivisions of any heading should be logically equivalent to that heading. For example:

I. Varieties of grapes

    A.   White grapes

    B.   Table grapes

    C.   Sweet juice grapes

Since two varieties (raisin grapes and canning grapes) are omitted, the outline is incomplete. The sum of the subheadings is not equal to the main heading. Such an error can be corrected in three ways:

a. Narrow the main heading, usually with a qualification like Major varieties or Some varieties.

b. Add the missing subheadings as D and E.

c. Add a miscellaneous category: D. Other varieties.

Arrangement
(Exercise K)

Determining the order in which headings should be arranged is usually less difficult than classification. If topics have been classified sensibly, their best arrangement is often unmistakable, and they fall into a natural, self-evident pattern. Sometimes, however, you need to ponder considerably and test various combinations to decide what order a reader can follow most easily. Each outline involves special problems, but the most common bases for arranging main topics and subtopics are the following:

1. **Time.** Many topics (for example, a battle, a process, a biographical episode) fall naturally into a chronological sequence. A plan based on time is usually easy for a reader to follow.
2. **Space.** A spatial arrangement (for example, near to far, right to left, east to west) should be maintained consistently and should be kept clear by adequate transitional phrasing.
3. **Logical relationship.** Arrangement may be based on an abstract relationship among ideas such as reasons for and against, definition, negative analysis, question and answer, cause and effect, comparison and contrast.
4. **Categories.** Some topics involve a ready-made division into groupings or types (for example, the kinds of sonnets, the major Protestant denominations, types of water pollutants, the Romance languages).

In arranging a series of topics not ordered by some obvious principle like time or space, consider two possibilities:

1. **Climax.** Especially in a series of ideas, it is often desirable to close with the

most important one. The final topic in a sequence is likely to impress itself on a reader's mind most forcibly.

2. **Coherence.** In making an outline, you should anticipate the paper that will be based on it. Sometimes you can facilitate transitions by placing a subtopic first when it relates to the close of the preceding section or by placing it last when it looks ahead to the beginning of the next one. Such linkage of parts is characteristic of good writing and is encouraged by thoughtful outlining. The sample paper (pp. 187–203) illustrates various ways of achieving coherence by arrangement.

Faulty Topic Outline
(Exercise L)

Some common violations of outlining conventions and logic are illustrated and identified in the faulty outline below.

Thesis: For widely different reasons, historical novels have been popular with American readers during three different periods.

I. 1820-1840

    A. Interest in Indians and the Frontier

illogical order → B. Sir Walter Scott was very popular and inspired American
(should be C)   *← faulty parallelism (sentence)*
       novelists.

    C. Patriotic pride in the new nation

    D. James Fenimore Cooper

        a. The Spy
        b. The Last of the Mohicans   *← inconsistent subdivision, wrong symbols*

II. 1890's

    A. Nationalism

       1. Result of Spanish-American War *← single division*

    B. Costume Romances

    C. Love of romantic adventure stories was not satisifed by
                         ← faulty parallelism (sentence)
       realistic fiction.

III. 1930's

    A. People wanted to escape economic worries. ← *faulty parallelism (sentence)*

    B. Reassurance from reading about past crises

    C. New interest in regional history and folklore

    D. <u>Gone</u> <u>with</u> <u>the</u> <u>Wind</u> ← *illogical division (overlaps A, B, C)*

IV. Some critical objections to historical novels

faulty parallelism (adjective) →

    A. Inaccuracy

    B. Often sentimental

    C. Melodramatic plots

    D. Influence of Hollywood ← *illogical division (overlaps A, B, C)*

← *illogical division since basis is chronological*

TYPES OF OUTLINES
(Exercises M and N)

The three types of formal outlines are illustrated on pages 87–90. The examples are identical in their basic content and differ only in form. The main headings are successful enterprises of P. T. Barnum, arranged in chronological order. Because the basis of division is consistent, the main topics do not overlap. A main topic like "Public gullibility" or "Barnum's autobiography" would impinge on all other main topics. The classification in I and III is based on cause and effect. In II and IV the main topics are divided into representative examples. The arrangement in I, II, and III is chronological. In IV it is generally chronological but also proceeds from the general to the specific.

The working outline would be considerably longer than the final outlines shown here. A final outline is intended for a reader and shows only salient points in the structure.

Obviously a reader would learn more about the content of the paper from the sentence outline than from either of the others. But this example also demonstrates a possible weakness of sentence outlines: they encourage the writing of sentences in similar form and of similar length—a common fault in mediocre prose.

The second example shows that a topic outline reveals very little of the substance of a paper. A topic outline is the skeleton of an essay—all bones and no flesh.

The combination form may be a desirable compromise. Writing each main topic as a sentence helps the writer judge whether it will unify that section of the essay. Phrases are sufficient to denote subtopics.

In practice, however, the form of the outline is not as important as its inherent logic. If you have a choice of forms, use whichever one seems best suited to your purpose and your writing habits.

Sample Sentence Outline

Thesis: P. T. Barnum's success as a showman was due to his genius for publicity and his shrewd knowledge of human nature.

I. His first successful exhibit was Joice Heth, billed as George Washington's nurse.

    A. Barnum placed advertisements in newspapers, and they reciprocated by printing long stories about the old woman.

    B. He gave her appearances religious and patriotic appeal by coaching her to sing hymns and tell anecdotes about Washington.

II. His American Museum, opened in 1842, exhibited a variety of attractions.

    A. Barnum distributed pictures and pamphlets to publicize a "mermaid," which was manufactured by a Japanese fisherman.

    B. Other popular exhibits included wild animals, performing fleas, giants, albinos, and a bearded lady.

    C. In 1842 he hired four-year-old Charles S. Stratton, renamed him General Tom Thumb, and exhibited him with great success in America and Europe.

    D. He stirred up public interest in Chang and Eng, the Siamese twins, by announcing that they planned to be separated by surgery.

III. In 1850 he paid Jenny Lind $150,000 to tour the United States.

    A. He arranged a huge reception for her arrival and conducted a contest to select the best welcoming poem.

    B. He created public interest by emphasizing her contributions to charities.

    C. The demand for tickets was so great that they were sold by auction.

IV. In 1871 he opened his circus, which ten years later became Barnum and Bailey.

    A. Because of public suspicion of circuses, especially the sideshows, he advertised it as the Great Moral Show.

    B. Each year he devised a new and larger opening spectacle, usually with a religious or patriotic theme.

C. In 1881 he purchased Jumbo, the world's largest elephant, from the London Zoo.

D. After Jumbo was killed in 1885, he exhibited its skelton and imported another elephant, billed as Alice, Jumbo's widow.

Sample Topic Outline

Thesis: P. T. Barnum's success as a showman was due to his genius for publicity and his shrewd knowledge of human nature.

I. Exhibition of Joice Heth

    A. Publicity

    B. Religious and patriotic appeal

II. The American Museum

    A. The Feejee Mermaid

    B. Other attractions

    C. General Tom Thumb

    D. Chang and Eng

III. Jenny Lind's tour

    A. Publicity concerning her arrival

    B. Emphasis on her charities

    C. Auction of tickets

IV. The circus

    A. Emphasis on morality in sideshows

    B. Religious and patriotic spectacles

    C. Jumbo, the world's largest elephant

    D. Alice, Jumbo's widow

Sample Combination Outline

Thesis: P. T. Barnum's success as a showman was due to his genius for publicity and his shrewd knowledge of human nature.

    I.   His first successful exhibit was Joice Heth, billed as George Washington's nurse.

        A. Publicity

        B. Religious and patriotic appeal

   II.   His American Museum, opened in 1842, exhibited a variety of attractions.

        A. The Fejee Mermaid

        B. Other attractions

        C. General Tom Thumb

        D. Chang and Eng

  III.   In 1850 he paid Jenny Lind $150,000 to tour the United States.

        A. Publicity concerning her arrival

        B. Emphasis on her charities

        C. Auction of tickets

   IV.   In 1871 he opened his circus, which ten years later became Barnum and Bailey.

        A. Emphasis on morality in sideshows

        B. Religious and patriotic spectacles

        C. Jumbo, the world's largest elephant

        D. Alice, Jumbo's widow

Exercise I   Classification: Specific to General

I. Classify the listed kitchen-items into three mutually exclusive groups. Write the numbers of items belonging to each group after one of the capital letters.

A _____

B _____

C _____

1. salad forks
2. thyme
3. cleaver
4. brown sugar
5. water glasses
6. blender
7. sirloin steak
8. paring knife
9. dried apricots
10. cookbook
11. green onions
12. soup bowls
13. rice

14. table cloth
15. rye bread
16. chafing dish
17. whipping cream
18. napkins
19. frying pan
20. measuring spoon
21. egg timer
22. coffee cups
23. spatula
24. instant coffee
25. cream pitcher
26. gravy

II. Classify the abbreviations in the running outline below into four mutually exclusive groups. After each capital letter, write the numbers of related items.

For the sake of consistency, all abbreviations are printed in full capitals and without periods, although usage is divided on some of them.

A _____

B _____

C _____

D _____

1. AEC   Atomic Energy Commission
2. AKA   also known as
3. APB   all-points bulletin
4. BB   bail bond
5. BCD   bad conduct discharge
6. BD   back dividends
7. BOB   Bureau of the Budget
8. CD   certificate of deposit
9. COD   cash on delivery
10. CPA   certified public accountant
11. CWO   chief warrant officer
12. D&D   drunk and disorderly
13. DPW   Director of Public Works
14. DWI   driving while intoxicated
15. FDIC   Federal Deposit Insurance Corporation
16. FHA   Federal Housing Administration
17. GHQ   General Headquarters
18. GTC   good till cancelled
19. IBM   International Business Machines
20. ICC   Interstate Commerce Commission
21. NYPD   New York Police Department
22. OD   officer of the day
23. PI   private investigator
24. SOB   Senate Office Building
25. WAAC   Women's Auxiliary Army Corps

Exercise J   Classification: General to Specific

Assume that the following sentence is the thesis for a paper on family names: *The original purpose of a surname was to identify an individual, usually by reference to occupation, appearance, family, or place of residence.*

A paper developing this thesis would obviously consist of four main divisions. Classify the names below into four mutually exclusive groups by writing the appropriate letter after each name.

A. Occupation
B. Appearance
C. Family relationship
D. Place of residence

If necessary, consult your dictionary for the meaning of Fitz-, Mac-, and O'-.

Armstrong	_____	Harper	_____
Atwater	_____	Klein	_____
Barber	_____	Longfellow	_____
Beard	_____	Longstreet	_____
Brown	_____	McBride	_____
Carpenter	_____	Miller	_____
Carter	_____	O'Brien	_____
Churchill	_____	Peterson	_____
Clark	_____	Rivera	_____
Cooper	_____	Smith	_____
Fitzgerald	_____	Taylor	_____
Ford	_____	Westfield	_____
Gardner	_____	Wheelwright	_____
Gross	_____	Whitehead	_____

Exercise K   Determining Arrangement

Determine a logical arrangement for the items in each group. Number the items above the line. State the principle on which you based each arrangement.

1. California   Kansas   Utah   Illinois   Ohio
    Basis of arrangement _____

2. copper   gold   platinum   silver
    Basis of arrangement _____

3. driving when intoxicated   double parking   speeding   leaving the scene of an accident
    Basis of arrangement _____

4. California   Maryland   Rhode Island   Texas   Alaska
    Basis of arrangement _____

5. Battle of North Africa   invasion of Europe   loss of the Philippines   dropping the atomic bomb   bombing of Pearl Harbor
    Basis of arrangement _____

6. tonsilitis   influenza   pneumonia   sinusitis
    Basis of arrangement _____

7. Silver Star   Purple Heart   Congressional Medal of Honor   Good Conduct Medal   Bronze Star
    Basis of arrangement _____

8. touchdown   safety   field goal   point after touchdown
    Basis of arrangement _____

9. Lee Harvey Oswald   Charles J. Guiteau   John Wilkes Booth   Leon Czolgosz
    Basis of arrangement _____

10. Mercury   Venus   Mars   Jupiter   Saturn
    Basis of arrangement _____

Exercise L   Analyzing a Faulty Outline

Analyze the following topic outline, which contains several errors. Write an X at the left side of each line that contains an error, and in the space on the right identify each error as is done in the example on pages 85–86.

Thesis: Because of his unusual personality and his eccentric behavior, John Chapman (Johnny Appleseed) is remembered in American folklore.

   I.   Legends of his early life

      A. Death of his sweetheart

      B. Injury to his head

      C. Arrived in Ohio

  II.   Planting apple trees

      A. Distribution of seedlings

      B. Location of orchards

         1. Protected slopes

      C. Trips to Pennsylvania for seeds

 III.   He wore strange costumes.

      A. Peculiar hats

      B. Cast-off coats

      C. Ummatched shoes

      D. Carelessness regarding appearance

  IV.   Diet

      A. Simple foods

         a. Milk and honey

         b. Mush

B. Refused to eat meat

V. Religion

A. Swedenborgian

Exercise M   Converting a Sentence Outline

Convert the sentence outline below to a topic outline or, if your instructor prefers, to a combination outline.

Thesis: During and after the Revolution, several artists made important contributions to the development of American painting.

I. Benjamin West lived in England from 1763 until his death in 1820.

   A. Although he was a patriotic American, he served as court painter to George III.

   B. He was President of the Royal Academy for twenty-seven years.

   C. He was a helpful friend to many American painters who visited England.

II. John Singleton Copley excelled in portraits and in historical paintings.

   A. His portraits reveal the character of his sitters.

   B. In England his most successful painting was Watson and the Shark, a dramatic scene in Havana Harbor.

   C. He painted several other narrative subjects.

III. Gilbert Stuart is best known for his portraits.

   A. In England (1775-88) he painted portraits of many public men, including George III.

   B. Though he went deeply in debt while living there, he painted successfully in Ireland (1788-93).

   C. From 1792 until his death in 1828, he lived in Boston and other American cities and painted portraits of Washington as well as other political and military leaders.

IV. Charles Willson Peale was the most versatile painter of his generation.

   A. Like Stuart he painted several portraits of Washington.

B. He also painted over 250 portraits of other Revolutionary leaders.

C. His scientific interests are shown in a large painting, Exhumation of the First American Mastodon.

D. In 1802 he founded the first American museum, where he displayed paintings, sculpture, and many scientific exhibits.

V. John Trumbull is best known for his historical paintings.

A. He painted many portraits and later incorporated some of them in historical scenes.

B. His historical murals were placed in the rotunda of the new Capitol.

C. In 1831 he gave his paintings to Yale, where they were displayed and studied in the first gallery devoted to an American artist.

Exercise N   Constructing an Outline

Each of the following summaries represents a major step in the development of an essay. Convert them into a topic outline with a thesis, main headings, and subtopics. Omit incidental details.

To the Greeks their gods were like persons. They resembled human beings in appearance. They also had human failings and human virtues.

Changes in power on Olympus were like earthly revolutions. Ge and Uranus were the first rulers. Cronus overthrew his father, Uranus, and seized power. Zeus, the son of Cronus, later overthrew him.

There were many legends of Zeus's love affairs with mortal women like Leda. Some of these stories resulted from the desire of ambitious families to claim divine ancestry. Others were invented by poets.

The gods exhibited human emotions. They were often jealous of each other. They sometimes felt fear, especially when Zeus was displeased. They were also proud, so that it was dangerous for a mortal to offend them.

The gods had many admirable characteristics. The patroness of Athens, Athena, represented wisdom and civilized life. Apollo taught men to know the divine will and to pacify the gods. Hestia, sister of Zeus, was the goddess of the hearth and a symbol of the home and family. Artemis, the goddess of the moon and sister to Apollo, protected young maidens.

FIVE
DOCUMENTING YOUR PAPER

Mark what ills the scholar's life assail.

In writing a research paper, you are free to use facts and opinions found in books and periodicals. You can use an author's actual language or you can summarize the ideas in your own words. In either case, you are obligated to document the borrowed material. Documentation—acknowledgment of indebtedness to a source—is of two general kinds: the *bibliography* and *notes*. The bibliography is a list of the sources used in a paper and is, thus, a blanket acknowledgment of indebtedness to each; *notes* (either footnotes or endnotes) acknowledge separately each borrowed fact or opinion.

THE PERILS OF PLAGIARISM

When you begin a paper, you may feel that you will need numerous notes, but since you do not credit to a single source facts that are common knowledge or opinions that are generally known and accepted, you will probably need fewer than you expect. Many facts and ideas that are new to you will appear in several discussions of your topic. If you express them in your own words, they ordinarily need not be cited in notes. But a fact or an opinion derived from a single source requires a citation note. An honest intention to give credit where credit is due and an understanding of the forms of documentation will keep you from the reality or the appearance of plagiarism (see also pp. 60–61).

Plagiarism (derived from a Latin word for kidnapper) means using another person's language or ideas without acknowledgment. Intentional plagiarism is a serious act of dishonesty that always carries a heavy penalty. Unfortunately, plagiarism can also be unintentional or accidental. It usually results from the careless omission of a citation note, failure to use quotation marks, or thoughtlessly echoing the language of a source. Be certain that whenever you borrow an author's phrasing you enclose it in quotation marks.

One of the most serious faults that can spoil a research paper is a style that alternates between student prose and the formal English of a reference book with no quotation marks to designate the latter. Anyone who writes develops a distinctive style, for better or for worse, and deviations from it are almost always obvious to a perceptive reader—one reason that handing in a ready-made paper purchased from a mail-order "writing service" is not only dishonest but dangerous.

As a rather grim analogy, copying a passage from a source without using quotation marks or a citation can be considered a felony. However, the numbered sentences below might charitably be considered misdemeanors. The first paraphrases the content, the second contains two borrowed phrases. Neither has a reference number to indicate a citation of the source. Much plagiarism is this sort of carelessness, but the penalty is often as severe as for deliberate copying from a source.

> Saul Bellow differs from most of his contemporaries in that he repudi-
> ates nihilistic despair, observes human existence from a comic perspec-
> tive, and concerns himself with fundamental moral and philosophical
> issues.

1. Unlike most American novelists, Saul Bellow is optimistic concerning man's destiny, has a lively sense of humor, and is interested in ideas.

2. Saul Bellow rejects the <u>nihilistic despair</u> of many of his contemporaries and views human behavior from his unique <u>comic perspective</u>.

To avoid any suggestion of plagiarism, copy a quotation note with meticulous care, enclose it in quotation marks, and compare it word by word with the source. Write a summary or an outline note from memory. Then compare it with the source to make certain that you have not inadvertently borrowed phrasing. If you borrow a key phrase, enclose it in quotation marks. Careful note-taking and conscientious documentation will enable you to fulfill your obligation to your sources and to your reader.

CONSISTENCY

Two facts about methods of documentation should be recognized at the outset: They are not foolproof, and they are not absolute. In almost every paper, a few problems arise that are not covered by any of the standard practices but require sensible improvisation. Improvised forms should be consistent with your practice elsewhere in the paper.

The form and the content of documentation are determined by conventions, not by rigid rules. Possibilities for variation are, therefore, almost limitless. So many minor variations are possible that documentation can become a nit-picker's nightmare and distract a writer's attention from more important matters like content, organization, and style.

The notes and the bibliography in a paper are intended to enable a reader to retrieve further information and should be simple, concise, and functional. Because there are several acceptable ways of arranging and punctuating notes and bibliographies, your practice must be consistent throughout a paper. For example, it is permissible to abbreviate names of states in notes; however, if you write *Pennsylvania* in one note, *Penna.* in another note, and *PA* in a third, two of the three must be considered faulty. It is sometimes better to be consistently wrong than to be right only part of the time. Next to simple carelessness, inconsistency is probably the most common fault in documentation.

The range of possible variations in documentation forms is suggested by the systems described in this chapter:

1. Conventional forms, recommended in style manuals published by the Modern Language Association (MLA) and in general use in the Humanities, are described and illustrated most fully. The examples can be adapted to any other system of documentation.
2. Forms used in the Natural and Social Sciences are illustrated and described briefly. No two fields use exactly the same system, and there are variations within every field. Because the system recommended by the American Psychological Association (APA style) is clearly and thoroughly described in a style manual, it is often used in Education and other fields, but even some journals in Psychology do not use APA style.
3. New forms were recommended by MLA in 1982 and have been used in *PMLA*, the journal of the association, since that time. The goals of the committee that studied scholarly procedures in the Humanities were "precision, accuracy, economy, consistency, and comprehensibility." The new system is much simpler than previous practice and undoubtedly is the future mode of documentation in the Humanities. Like the before-and-after pictures in advertisements for hair coloring or diet pills, two versions of the sample paper (pp. 184–226), one using conventional forms and the other using new MLA forms, illustrate differences between the two styles of documentation.

Do not be intimidated by the numerous examples in the next two sections. If you master basic bibliography and note forms for a book and for a magazine, you can adapt them to most special situations as they arise.

CONVENTIONAL STYLE IN THE HUMANITIES

Inconsistency never can be right.

This section describes bibliography and note forms in general use in the Humanities. A few major variations are included and are designated by the word *variant* in the margin. If your instructor prefers that you use one of the variant forms, star the example of that form and follow it consistently. If two examples are given and neither is labeled *variant*, they are equally acceptable.

This is an appropriate time to review the Checklist on page vii and to make certain that you know your instructor's preference on the following questions (15–20):

> Notes and bibliography: Footnotes or endnotes?
> Each entry single- or double-spaced?
> Publisher included?
> Arabic or Roman numerals for volumes?
> Military style for dates?
> New MLA forms?
> Display quotations: Single- or double-spaced?
> Latin words and abbreviations: Underlined or not?

BIBLIOGRAPHY
(Exercise O)

A bibliography is an alphabetical list of sources of information. In preparing your research paper, you keep a card file of the sources that you use and list those sources at the end of your paper.

Kinds of Bibliographies

1. **Bibliographies compiled by others.** In many textbooks and reference works, sources that the author has used will be listed at the end of each chapter or as an appendix. Bibliographies on special subjects are also published separately in book or pamphlet form. As a guide to useful sources, such listings can be very helpful. Because of the many different bibliographical styles, you must be certain that you convert a reference to the form that you are following in your own bibliography. Especially useful is the annotated or critical bibliography, which includes an indication of the content of a source and a brief judgment of its value.
2. **Bibliographies compiled by yourself.** Students are occasionally required to

assemble a list of sources dealing with a particular subject. Although such an assignment is more common in advanced courses, it is sometimes used in an introductory course to acquaint students with library resources and scholarly procedures. More often, a student records the books and periodicals consulted during the preparation of a paper. This list of references is the final page of a paper.

In most papers, the bibliography is a single alphabetical list. If you have an unusually large number of sources, you can divide them into separately alphabetized sections, such as Books and Periodicals, Primary Sources and Secondary Sources, or Books and Films.

The bibliographical description of a source includes all information necessary to identify it. For a librarian, a rare book dealer, or a professional bibliographer, this includes the size, the binding, and other technical details. In a simple bibliography for a research paper, three major items are necessary: the author, the title, and the facts of publication. The examples below illustrate a variety of bibliographical entries, all of them following that basic pattern.

Examples

To illustrate all possible variations in bibliographical forms would be impossible. The numbered examples on the following pages cover most of the problems that you will encounter and can serve as models. When you compile your bibliography, if a source is somehow out of the ordinary, use the checklist below to locate an example that resembles your source. The first number after each item in the checklist designates the basic example. Other numbers, if any, indicate additional examples that illustrate the same type of form.

Checklist of Bibliographic Forms

Anonymous work **3** 22,23,38	Multiple authorship **21**
Anthology **4** 32	Newspaper **22**
Book, standard form **1** 40	Pamphlet **23**
Collaborator **5**	Personal letter **24**
Corporate author **6**	Photocopy **25**
Edition **7** 9	Pseudonym **26**
Editor **8** 4,23,28,31,32,33,36	Public document **27**
Encyclopedia **9**	Published letter **28**
Film **10**	Recording or cassette **29**
Filmstrip **11**	Reprint **30**
Illustrator **12**	Review **31**
Interview **13**	Selection in anthology **32**
Introduction **14** 12	Series **33** 21,30
Joint authorship **15**	Subtitle **34** 4,5,8,14,21,32,36,39
Lecture **16**	Television or radio program **35**
Legal reference **17**	Title within a title **36** 18
Magazine continuously paged **18** 2,15,28,36	Translation **37**
	Untitled article **38**
Magazine, standard form **2**	Volume number **39** 2,9,15,18,25,28,30,34,36
Manuscript materials **19**	
Microforms **20**	Works by the same author **40**

Standard Forms

The order and the punctuation of standard forms for a book and for a magazine are as follows:

Book: Author. *Title*. Place: Publisher, Year.
Magazine: Author. "Title." *Magazine,* Volume (Issue), Pages.

Thus, a bibliographical entry consists of three basic items (author, title, and facts of publication), each followed by a period. If you maintain the same sequence of items, omit information that is not available or not pertinent and add supplementary information like an editor's name or the name of a series when it is relevant, you should have little difficulty in devising sensible forms for any unusual sources.

1. Book, Standard Form _____

yes → Bernard, Jessie. <u>The Female World</u>. New York: Free Press, 1981.

variant ⁿᵒ Bernard, Jessie. <u>The Female World</u>. New York, 1981.

ⁿᵒ *variant*   **1.** Single-space each entry; double-space between entries. However, your instructor may prefer that you double-space throughout—customary practice in a manuscript that is to be printed.

2. Reverse or hanging indentation (five spaces) makes it easier for a reader to locate an item in an alphabetized list.

3. The author's name is inverted for alphabetization. It should be written as it appears on the title page: Salinger, J. D., not Salinger, Jerome David.

4. Copy the title from the title page, not from the cover or the spine of a book. The title of a book (or of any other published unit) is underlined. Underlining in a manuscript is the equivalent of italics in a printed work. Underlining a title word by word is sometimes recommended, perhaps because it is more trouble: <u>A</u> <u>Tale</u> <u>of</u> <u>Two</u> <u>Cities</u>, but underlining continuously is also *variant* acceptable: <u>A Tale of Two Cities</u>. What really matters is that your practice be consistent throughout a paper.

5. If more than one city is listed on the title page, cite the first one. Do not include the state for major cities. After the name of a city, abbreviate a state if it is spelled with more than four letters. Do not abbreviate a city or a state in the text of your paper or in the name of a university press.

6. The name of a publishing firm can be shortened, at least to the extent of omitting words like "Publishers" and abbreviations like "Co." or "Inc." The word "Press" is usually retained to avoid ambiguity. Do not use an ampersand (&) unless it is part of the official name of the firm.

7. Use the year of publication on the title page if one appears there. Otherwise, look on the reverse of the title page, where you may find a confusing jumble of years (see the reverse of the title page in this manual). If there are several copyright dates, use the most recent one. If there have been several printings of the edition you are using, use the date of the earliest one.

variant
The second form above, which omits the publisher, may be adequate in a short paper if your instructor approves. It is also sometimes considered permissible to omit the publisher for a book published before 1900.

2. Magazine, Standard Form _____

Drew, Elizabeth. "A Political Journal." <u>New Yorker</u>, 26 Sept. 1983, pp. 140-49.

Kuttner, Bob. "The Declining Middle." <u>Atlantic Monthly</u>, July 1983, pp. 60-72.

Kiernan, Bernard. "The Conservative Illusion." <u>Virginia Quarterly Review</u>, 59 (Spring 1983), 208-22.

1. The title of an article (like all *portions* of published units) is enclosed in quotation marks. The name of a magazine is underlined. An initial "The" (as in <u>The New Yorker</u>) can be dropped.

2. The examples above illustrate entries for a weekly, a monthly, and a quarterly magazine. The order is the same in all of them: Author. Title. Publication Facts.

3. The volume number is not necessary for a recent issue of a weekly or monthly magazine but is always cited for a quarterly. Arabic numerals are preferable to Roman because they are less cumbersome. Be consistent throughout a paper.

4. When a volume number is cited, it is not followed by a comma, the issue date is *variant* enclosed in parentheses, and the abbreviation "pp." is omitted. Since the quarterly is continuously paged (see Example 18 below), the year alone would be sufficient.
5. Military style (day-month-year) is the simplest way of writing dates. Months of more than four letters are usually abbreviated.
6. Inclusive page numbers below 100 are cited in full: 60–72. In numbers greater than 100 and in the same 100, only the last two figures of the second number are cited: 208–22, but 163–207.

3. Anonymous Work

A Critical Fable. Boston: Houghton Mifflin, 1922.

variant [Lowell, Amy]. A Critical Fable. Boston: Houghton Mifflin, 1922.

Anonymous, M.D. The Healers. New York: Putnam, 1967.

"Coping with Nature." Time, 29 Aug. 1983, pp. 10–11.

An anonymous work is alphabetized by the first word of its title other than an article (a, an, the). If you identify an author, as in the second example, enclose the name in brackets but alphabetize the work by its title. If the author's identity is significant in the paper, it will undoubtedly be discussed there, and the value of including it in the bibliography seems questionable. Do not use the word "Anonymous" unless it appears on the title page of the work, as is the case in the third example.

4. Anthology

Cohen, Sara Blacker, ed. From Hester Street to Hollywood: The Jewish-American Stage and Screen. Bloomington, Ind.: Indiana Univ. Press, 1983.

When an anthology is cited as a unit, the implication is that two or more selections are used in the paper. For an illustration of an entry citing a single selection in an anthology, see Example 32.

5. Collaborator

Haldeman, H. R. The Ends of Power. With Joseph DiMona. New York: Times Books, 1978.

Hoffa, James R. Hoffa: The Real Story. As Told to Oscar Fraley. New York: Stein and Day, 1975.

Autobiographical books by nonliterary celebrities are often produced with professional assistance, which is acknowledged, if at all, by a phrase like those used above, "Editorial Assistance by," or "In Collaboration with." Cite the collaborator by using whatever phrase appears on the title page.

6. Corporate Author

National Council of Teachers of English. <u>Idea Exchange for English Teachers</u>. Urbana, Ill.: NCTE, 1983.

<u>Idea Exchange for English Teachers</u>. By National Council of Teachers of English. Urbana, Ill.: NCTE, 1983.

Either of these forms is acceptable for a work in which an institution, a committee, or some other group is designated as author on the title page. NCTE, written without periods, is the accepted abbreviation for the name of the organization. Since the name is cited in full in the author-position, spelling it out a second time as publisher seems unnecessary.

7. Edition

Borklund, Elmer. <u>Contemporary Literary Criticism</u>. 2nd ed. Detroit: Gale, 1982.

Ellman, Richard. <u>James Joyce</u>. Rev. ed. New York: Oxford Univ. Press, 1982.

Be certain to cite the date of the edition that you are using, not the date of the original copyright.

8. Editor

Saroyan, William. <u>My Name Is Saroyan</u>. Ed. James H. Tashjian. New York: Coward-McCann, 1983.

Roy, Maria, ed. <u>The Abusive Partner: An Analysis of Domestic Battery</u>. New York: Van Nostrand Reinhold, 1983.

Usage is divided regarding the positon of an editor's name, but the author of a work edited by someone else should ordinarily be cited first.

9. Encyclopedia

"Satire." <u>Encyclopaedia Britannica: Macropaedia</u> (1974).

"Satire." <u>Encyclopedia Americana</u>. 1976 ed.

variant "Satire." <u>Encyclopedia Americana</u>. 1976 ed. 24, 294-95.

variant Holman, C. Hugh. "Satire." Encyclopedia Americana. 1976 ed.

variant R[obert] C. E[lliott]. "Satire." Encyclopaedia Britannica. Macropaedia. 1974 ed.

The first two forms above are adequate because only the topic is needed to locate an article in a reference work that is alphabetically arranged. The place of publication and the publisher are usually omitted from citations of standard encyclopedias. The two ways of indicating the edition used are illustrated in the first two examples. Citing the volume and pages is a somewhat gratuitous courtesy to the reader. The author's name is not helpful in locating an article but may be significant for other reasons. Major articles in the *Americana* are signed in full. Articles in the *Macropaedia* volumes of *Britannica III* are signed with initials, which are identified in the index volume (*Propaedia*).

10. Film

Beresford, Bruce, dir. Tender Mercies. Prod. Philip S. Hobel. With Robert Duvall and Tess Harper. Universal Studios, 1983.

Tender Mercies. Dir. Bruce Beresford. Universal Studios, 1983.

Considerable variation is possible in the documentation of a film, depending on what aspects are significant in a paper. The title, the director, the distributor, and the year are the basic items. If a film is merely mentioned in a paper, documentation is unnecessary. If its content or some aspect of its production is discussed, it should be documented. In a paper considering several films, it would be advisable to list them in a subsection of the bibliography.

11. Filmstrip

Mythology Lives! (filmstrip). Mount Kisco, N.Y.: Center for Humanities, 1983.

Joyce and Beckett. Princeton, N.J.: Films for the Humanities, 1983. (Filmstrip FFH 353.)

The medium (filmstrip) can be designated immediately after the title or at the close. If an order number is included as in the second example, putting it at the close is preferable.

12. Illustrator

Stapledon, Olaf. Nebular Maker & Four Encounters. Introd. Arthur C. Clark. Illus. Jim Stalin. New York: Dodd, Mead, 1983.

Unless the illustrations are discussed in the paper, this item of information might be omitted from a simple bibliography. The ampersand is part of the title and, therefore, should not be changed to "and."

13. Interview _____

Bates, Horace J. Personal interview. Memphis, Tenn., 18 Mar. 1984.

Fuller, Mary. Telephone interview. 12 Jan. 1984.

The name of the person interviewed, the mode of communication, and the date are the essential items.

14. Introduction _____

Rogosin, Donn. *Invisible Men: Life in Baseball's Negro Leagues.*
    Introd. Monte Irvin. New York: Anthaneum, 1983.

Irvin, Monte, introd. *Invisible Men: Life in Baseball's Negro Leagues.*
    By Donn Rogosin. New York: Antheneum, 1983.

The distinction between the two forms above is that in the first one the introduction is merely part of the bibliographical description and in the second it is used in the paper. If both the introduction and the book were used in the paper, the first form would be appropriate. The author of an introduction is not designated as the editor of a work unless such a designation appears on the title page.

15. Joint Authorship _____

Chancellor, John, and Walter R. Mears. *The News Business.* New York:
    Harper & Row, 1983.

Weisberg, Herbert I., and Thomas J. Tomberlin. "Statistical Evidence in
    Employment Discrimination Cases." *Statistical Methods & Reseach,*
    11 (May 1983), 381-406.

The order of names on the title page should always be followed. A work will usually be cataloged or indexed under each author's name, but it will always be listed under the name of the first author. Only the first author's name is inverted. The comma after the given name (John, Herbert I.,) is standard, though not altogether logical.

16. Lecture _____

Pickett, Mary W. Public lecture, "The Rights of Minorities." Memphis,
    Tenn., 27 Oct. 1983.

Murphy, George. Class lecture, Sociology 402. Westminister College.
    17 Jan. 1984.

The speaker, the title if any, the place, and the date are the basic facts.

17. Legal Reference _____

Railroad Retirement Act of 1937. 10 U.S. Code. Title 45, Secs.
      228a-228z. Washington, D.C.: GPO, 1971.

Brown v. General Services Administration et al. 425 U.S. Reports
      820-39. No. 74-768. U.S. Sup. Ct. 1976.

United States v. Marvin Mandel et al. 408 Federal Supplement 673-79.
      St. Paul, Minn.: West, 1976. U.S. Dist. Ct. Maryland. 1975.

Laws and legal cases are even more varied and more formidably complicated than public documents (see Example 27). Lawyers and legal writers use a system of abbreviations that seems like a secret code to most laymen; expand these abbreviations when necessary for clarity. Cite the title of a law, the volume number of the statute book, the title, and the sections. Page numbers are not necessary. *United States Code* is generally abbreviated as *U.S.C.* or *USC.* The publisher (GPO) might be omitted. Because legal reference works run into so many volumes and are constantly increasing, Roman numerals can be rather complex (CDXXV); therefore, Arabic numerals (425) are preferable. For a legal case, cite the parties to the suit, the volume number and the title and the pages of the source, the name of the court, and the year the case was decided. You can use official court reports or compilations by a commercial publisher like the third example above. In actual practice you are likely to use a discussion of a case in a source; you would then document that source like any other book. A minor oddity is that names of cases are underlined in the text of a paper but not in documentation; names of laws or acts are not underlined or enclosed in quotation marks.

18. Magazine Continuously Paged _____

Flax, Neil M. "The Presence of the Sign in Goethe's Faust." PMLA, 98
      (1983), 183-203.

Most scholarly journals are paginated continuously throughout a volume, and so the issue need not be designated. In actual practice, however, a reader using unbound copies of the periodical would have to guess at the issue containing the designated pages. Specifying the issue (Mar. 1983) is very little trouble and seems advisable.

19. Manuscript Materials _____

Faulkner, William. Letter to Morton Goldman. 18 July 1935. Arents
      Coll. New York Public Library.

Melville, Herman. Journal for August 1860. Papers and Library of the
      Melville Family. Harvard Library.

Worthie, Peleg. Diary 1862-65. (Two manuscript notebooks owned by the Worthie Family, Newton, Ohio.)

Holsberry, John Edwin, Jr. "Hawthorne and the English Romantic Poets." Diss. Duke 1976.

In a short paper you are not likely to use unpublished letters, diaries, or other manuscript materials, but if you do, it is important to conform as closely as possible to normal bibliographical order. Your basic purpose is to identify the source and its location. Include any special designations used by the repository of the materials: for example, Folder 6, Drawer 2, or Notebook 31. The fourth example above is the only one with an actual title. The title of any unpublished work, regardless of its length, is enclosed in quotation marks.

20. Microform _____

Mitchell, D. H. "Mushrooms," Mycology, No. 1. Denver: Poisindex, 1974. (Microfiche.)

Usage has not been standardized for documenting the various types of microforms. The simplest procedure is to follow the form for a book as closely as possible and to identify the type of microform at the close. If the reproduction is simply a substitute version of the original (e.g., the *New York Times* on microfilm), document it as you would the original. It is not necessary to identify it as microfilm.

21. Multiple Authorship _____

Krasnow, Erwin G., Lawrence D. Longley, and Herbert A. Terry. The Politics of Broadcast Regulation. New York: St. Martin's Press, 1982.

variant Shafritz, Jay M., Walter L. Balk, Albert C. Hyde, and David H. Rosenbloom. Personnel Management in Government: Politics and Process. Publications in Public Administration and Public Policy. New York: Marcel Dekker, 1978.

Shafritz, Jay M., and others. Personnel Management in Government: Politics and Process. Publications in Public Policy. New York: Marcel Dekker, 1978.

If a work has three authors or editors, all three are cited. If there are four or *variant* more, only the first is necessary. The Latin abbreviation "*et al.*" would be acceptable in the third example, but the English "and others" is more commonly used. Note that the name of a series is not underlined.

22. Newspaper _____

<u>Evening Sun</u> [Baltimore], 2-7 Oct. 1983.

variant   Baltimore <u>Evening Sun</u>, 2-7 Oct. 1983.

"Senators Disclose Arms Limit Proposal." <u>Atlanta Constitution</u>,
     12 Sept. 1983, A, p. 2.

Green, Larry. "Chicago May Say 'Whoa' to Horsy Set." <u>Los Angeles
     Times</u>, 10 Sept. 1983, Part I, p. 14.

"Clean Air Costs." Editorial. <u>Washington Post</u>, 12 Aug. 1983, Sec. A,
     p. 16.

Baker, Russell. "This Garrulous Silence." <u>New York Times</u>, 14 Sept.
     1983, p. 23.

These examples illustrate a continuing news story (Specific issues used would be identified in citation notes.), an unsigned news story, a signed news story, an editorial, and a syndicated column. The name of the city is underlined if it appears as part of the name of the newspaper on the front page. Otherwise, it precedes the name but is not underlined or, preferably, follows the name and is bracketed as in the first example. In many newspapers each section is paged separately, and so the section must be cited. Use the designation found in the newspaper. The column number (counted from the left-hand side of the page) may also be included after the page number, but this seems unnecessary in a short bibliography.

23. Pamphlet _____

Dickman, Irving R. <u>Behavior Modification</u>. New York: Public Affairs
     Committee, 1976.

Dittrich, Kathinka, and Henry Marx, eds. <u>Cultural Guide for Berlin</u>.
     n.p.: n.p., n.d.

<u>Why You Can Count on Cotton</u>. Memphis, Tenn.: National Cotton Council,
     n.d.

<u>Eating for Better Health</u>. Washington, D.C.: GPO, 1981.

As the first two examples illustrate, the available publication data for a pamphlet may range from all to none. Follow the normal order for a book entry and omit whatever is unavailable. The abbreviation "n.p." means "no place of publication" when it appears on the left side of the colon and "no publisher" when it appears on the right side. The abbreviation "n.d.", of course, means "no date."

24. Personal Letter

```
Pynchon, Thomas. Personal letter. 9 June 1984.
```

A letter can also be cited as "Letter to the author," which in the above example would be slightly ambiguous. The abbreviations "ALS" (autograph letter signed) and "TLS" (typed letter signed) seem unnecessary in a short paper.

25. Photocopy

```
Skaggs, Merrill Maguire. "Poe's Longing for a Bicameral Mind." Southern
     Quarterly, 19 (Winter 1981), 54-64. (Photocopy.)
```

You may use a photocopy of an article or a portion of a book, especially if you obtain it from another library through interlibrary loan. You can designate it "Photocopy" as is done above, but it is also permissible simply to document it as you would the original.

26. Pseudonym

```
Nasby, Petroleum V. [David Ross Locke]. The Nasby Papers. Indianapolis:
     C. O. Perrine, 1864.

Nasby, Petroleum V. [Pseud.] The Nasby Papers. Indianapolis: C. O.
     Perrine, 1864.
```

If you need the actual name of an author writing under a pseudonym, you can find it in a library card catalog or in a dictionary of pseudonyms. To identify a well-known pseudonym like Mark Twain or O. Henry or to follow it with [Pseud.] seems pedantic and unnecessary. Note the use of brackets.

27. Public Document

```
U.S.H.R. "Panama Canal Authorization, Fiscal Year 1982." Report No.
     97-64. In House Reports, Nos. 59-90. 97th Cong., 1st sess.
     Washington, D.C.: GPO, 1981.

U.S.H.R. Committee on Ways and Means. Caribbean Basin Initiative. 97th
     Cong., 2nd sess. Washington, D.C.: GPO, 1982.

U.S. Office of Management and Budget. Budget of the United States
     Government, Fiscal Year 1983. Washington, D.C.: GPO, 1983.

Coral Gables, Fla. Annual Financial Report. Coral Gables, Fla.:
     Finance Dept., 1980.
```

U.S. Cong. Rec. (Daily). 15 Sept. 1983, pp. S12313-14.

U.S. Cong. Rec. Vol. 121, Part 32, 18 Dec. 1975, pp. 41843-44.

Federal, state, county, and city govenments issue an incredible variety of documents: bills, statutes, regulations, statistics, hearings, reports, proceedings, executive orders, speeches, and many others. They vary greatly in form, and documentation often presents problems. The government and the agency issuing a document usually come first, followed by the title and whatever information is needed to identify and locate it. As with legal documents, volume numbers are often long, and so Arabic numerals are simpler to use and to interpret. Abbreviations are used freely in citations. "GPO" is a standard abbreviation for "Government Printing Office," as is "Cong. Rec." for the *Congressional Record.*

Reports of Congressional hearings often contain valuable material, but searching it out requires patience. The basic order of a citation is the name of the committee, the title of the report, the number and session of Congress. Reports of lengthy hearings are published piecemeal in pamphlets, which are combined in bound volumes after the hearings are completed. Use the bound volumes whenever possible, because most libraries store or discard the pamphlets after receiving the bound volumes. The first example is a brief report in a bound collection; the second is a separate publication.

The *Congressional Record* illustrates some of the inconsistencies that create problems when you use public documents. It is a record of Congressional proceedings augmented by any material that a member requests be "read into the record." It is published each day that Congress is in session and then is republished in bound volumes, which inconveniently do not correspond to the original issues in content or in pagination. The page numbers in the examples above suggest the scope of this source. A practical way of using it is to determine the date of a speech or a debate by consulting the *New York Times Index* and then to examine the issue for that date. Whenever possible, use the bound volumes because few libraries retain the daily issues after receiving the bound volumes or microfilm reproductions.

28. Published Letter

Saxon, A. H., ed. Selected Letters of P. T. Barnum. New York: Columbia Univ. Press, 1983.

Barnard, Ellsworth. Letter. "The Language of Criticism." PMLA, 98 (1983), 87.

Specific letters used from the source in the first example would be designated in citation notes (see Notes, Example 28). The second example above is a letter to the editor. The heading was supplied by the journal and is treated as a title. When no such heading appears, just the word "Letter" is used without quotation marks. *PMLA* is the actual title of the journal (*Publications of the Modern Language Association*) and is written without periods. Since *PMLA* is paginated consecutively throughout the year, the specific issue is not necessary (see Example 18).

29. Recording or Cassette

Halbreich, Harry. Jacket Notes. Symphony No. 1 in D Major. By Gustav
    Mahler. Cond. Erich Leinsdorf, Royal Philharmonic Orchestra.
    London Records, SMAS 94801, 1972.

Mahler, Gustav. Symphony No. 1 in D Major. Cond. Erich Leinsdorf, Royal
    Philharmonic Orchestra. Jacket notes by Harry Halbreich. London
    Records, SMAS 94801, 1972.

Eliot, T. S. "The Wasteland." Caedmon Treasury of Modern Poets.
    Caedmon, TC2006A, n.d.

Dropping Out: Road to Nowhere. Center for Humanities, Video casette
    V-6793-3070, 1983.

The first form above would be suitable if you quoted from the jacket notes in your paper. In the second example, the jacket notes are merely part of the bibliographical description and are not strictly necessary. If you simply mention a musical composition in a paper, it is not necessary to document it. But if the subject of your paper is some aspect of music and you refer to several recordings, you should list them in a subsection of the bibliography. The title of a musical composition is not underlined if it merely identifies it by form, number, and key (cf. *La Traviata*).

30. Reprint

Wendell, Barrett. A Literary History of America. 1900; rpt. New York:
    Haskell House, 1968.

Mayhew, Henry. London Labour and the London Poor. 4 vols. London,
    1861-62; rpt. New York: Dover, 1968.

variant Mayhew, Henry. London Labour and the London Poor. 4 vols. Rpt. New
    York: Dover, 1968. (Orig. publ. London, 1861-62.)

variant Bronte, Emily. Wuthering Heights (1847). Riverside Editions. Boston:
    Houghton Mifflin, 1956.

The first two examples illustrate the most common way of citing a reprinted work. The city is included with the year for works published outside the United States. If your paper deals with a literary classic, you will probably mention its year of publication in discussing it; if not, you could indicate the year as is done in the last example.

31. Review

Rev. of Pandora's Box. New Yorker, 19 Sept. 1983, p. 30.

D. O. Rev. of The Oxford Book of Death, ed. by D. J. Enright. Harper's,
    Aug. 1983, p. 75.

Schlesinger, Arthur M. Jr. "Requiem for Neoliberalism." Rev. of A New
    Democracy, by Gary Hart. New Republic, 6 June 1983, pp. 28-30.

Crist, Judith. "Bergman's Rosetta Stone." Rev. of Fanny and Alexander.
    Saturday Review, May-June 1983, pp. 41-42.

A review may be anonymous as in the first example or signed with initials as in the second example. Reviews are often untitled as in the first two examples. The word "Review" should be spelled out if there is any possibility that it might be confused with "Revision." Note that it is not enclosed in quotation marks because it is not a title. The first and fourth examples are reviews of films; the second and third are reviews of books. The same basic form can be used for reviews of plays, concerts, or any other type of performance.

32. Selection in Anthology

Brater, Enoch. "Ethnics and Ethnicity in the Plays of Arthur Miller."
    In From Hester Street to Hollywood: The Jewish-American Stage and
    Screen. Ed. Sarah Blacker Cohen. Bloomington, Ind.: Indiana Univ.
    Press, 1983, pp. 123-36.

To cite a single selection from an anthology, begin with the author's name. For the citation of an entire anthology, see Example 4.

33. Series

Matzer, John, Jr., ed. Capital Financing Strategies for Local
    Governments. Practical Management Series. Washington, D.C.:
    International City Management Assn., 1983.

The title of a series follows the title of the book and is not underlined.

34. Subtitle

Sundquist, Eric J. Faulkner: The House Divided. Baltimore: Johns
    Hopkins Univ. Press, 1983.

Benedict, Helen. "Bernard Malamud: Morals and Surprises." Antioch
    Review, 41 (Winter 1983), 28-36.

The use of subtitles for both books and articles appears to be increasing. A subtitle should be included in a bibliography but can be omitted from notes (see Notes, Example 34). A colon is used to introduce a subtitle even though no colon appears in the original. The first word after the colon and subsequent words except articles and prepositions are capitalized.

35. Television or Radio Program _____

Arthur C. Clarke's Mysterious World. PBS TV. 20 Oct. 1983.

Rather, Dan. CBS Evening News. CBS TV. 9 Nov. 1983.

Larry King Show. WGBS Radio. 4 Oct. 1983.

The basic items of information are the name of the program, the network or station, and the date.

36. Title within a Title _____

Ringler, Ellin. "Middlemarch: A Feminist Perspective." Studies in the
     Novel, 15 (Spring 1983), 55-61.

Ruddick, Lisa. "'Melanctha' and the Psychology of William James."
     Modern Fiction Studies, 28 (Winter 1982-83), 545-56.

"The American Scholar" Today: Emerson's Essay and Some Critical Views.
     Ed. C. David Mead. New York: Dodd, Mead, 1970.

Mandel, Oscar. Annotations to Vanity Fair. Washington, D.C.: University
     Press of America, 1981.

variant Mandel, Oscar. Annotations to "Vanity Fair." Washington, D.C.: University Press of America, 1981.

These examples illustrate the possible combinations in which one title can appear within another title. When the title of an article contains the title of a book, the book title is underlined. When the title of an article contains a title in double quotation marks, they are changed to singles. When the title of a book contains a quoted title, the quotation marks are retained. When the title of a book contains a book title, the second or shorter title is not underlined or, less often, is enclosed in quotation marks.

37. Translation

Beauvoir, Simone de. <u>When Things of the Spirit Come First</u>. Trans. Patrick O'Brien. New York: Pantheon, 1982.

variant Lattimore, Richard, trans. <u>The Iliad of Homer</u>. Chicago: Univ. of Chicago Press, 1962.

The name of a translator ordinarily follows the title of a work. The second form might be used to distinguish a particular version of a work that has been translated many times.

38. Untitled Article

<u>Time</u>. 19 Sept. 1983, p.82.

Articles without some form of title or heading are uncommon, but if you cite one you should follow basic bibliographical form and omit whatever is unavailable. This example refers to a paragraph in the "People" section of *Time*. Citing "People" as the title would be of no assistance to a reader.

39. Volume Number

Blotner, Joseph. <u>Faulkner: A Biography</u>. New York: Random House, 1974. Vol. 2.

Edel, Leon. <u>Henry James</u>. 5 vols. Philadelphia: Lippincott, 1953-72.

Edel, Leon. <u>The Treacherous Years: 1895-1901</u>. Vol. 4 of <u>Henry James</u>. Philadelphia: Lippincott, 1969.

When you use only part of a multivolume work, indicate at the end of the entry the volume or volumes actually used. If you use all the volumes in a multivolume work, indicate the number of volumes after the title. If each volume has a separate title and publication date, indicate the volume number before the title of the complete work. If you use more than one volume in such a source, cite each in a separate entry. Designation of a volume number is one of the few remaining uses of Roman numerals, and even here Arabic numerals are more common. Roman numerals *variant* could be used in the first and third examples: (Vol. II, Vol. IV).

40. Works by Same Author

Bellow, Saul. <u>Mr. Sammler's Planet</u>. New York: Viking, 1970.

_____. <u>Humboldt's Gift</u>. New York: Viking, 1975.

_____. The Dean's December. New York: Harper & Row, 1982.

variant   When you list more than one work by the same author, substitute a line ten spaces long (or the same number of spaces as the author's last name) for the name in the second and successive entries. This device is used only in bibliographies. Ditto marks are never used in documentation. Such entries can be arranged alphabetically by title or chronologically. In a paper discussing some phase of an author's career, chronological order would be more appropriate.

NOTES

A list of the sources used in a paper, the bibliography is a general acknowledgment of indebtedness. Notes specify the particular portions of each source that have been used. Whether written at the bottom of each page as footnotes or on a separate page at the end of the paper as endnotes (sometimes called backnotes), the form and the purpose are the same.

Notes supply a reader with specific citations of sources and with supplementary information. Because the punctuation and content of notes are variable conventions rather than rigid rules, consistency is all-important. It is also important to remember that notes are a convenience to the reader, not a display of the extent of your research. Some student papers contain too many notes; some, too few. Either extreme can be a serious fault. If you are in doubt about the need for a particular note, consult your instructor.

Uses

Notes have four general uses:

1. **Citation.** These notes identify the precise source of borrowed material. The purpose of a citation note is to enable readers to locate the original source if they want to investigate a topic more fully or verify a statement. You will, of course, use citation notes in your research paper.
2. **Explanation.** These notes contain information that pertains to some aspect of a topic but is not directly relevant to the thesis. They are used in printed works to conserve space. In student research papers, they should be used sparingly, but they can be a convenient way of identifying individuals or defining terms.
3. **Reference.** These notes may direct the reader to another page of the paper or, more often, to other sources that either corroborate or contradict a statement. They are usually introduced by "See also" or "Compare." They are not often used in student papers, but reference notes in a book or an article can be useful leads to other sources.
4. **Combination.** Any or all of the above kinds of notes can be combined. Examples of combination notes appear in the sample paper (pp. 204–06).

Numbering and Placement

From observation you undoubtedly have already learned the basic procedure of writing notes. An index numeral, elevated a half space,[1] is placed *after* the passage to which it refers and after any punctuation mark except a dash. A corresponding numeral, also elevated and followed by a space, is placed before the note. This numeral is called a *superscript.* Notes should be numbered consecutively throughout a paper. Arabic numerals should be used except after statistics or other numerical data, where an asterisk (*) may be used to avoid confusion. If your paper contains more than one collection of statistics, it is advisable to use additional asterisks rather than other typewritten characters like #, %, or ¢.

Whenever a research paper is assigned, some students devise ingenious locations for notes, such as the facing left-hand page with arrows pointing to the text or paper tabs taped to the page. The two acceptable positions, however, are at the bottom of the page and on separate pages after the text of the paper and before the bibliography. Writing endnotes is much simpler and has become the more common practice. In a manuscript that is to be printed, this procedure is mandatory because notes are set in type as a separate operation. A page is usually headed "Notes," and the notes are numbered consecutively to match the numbers appearing in the text. Endnotes are used in the sample paper (pp. 205–07). For an illustration of a page with footnotes, see page 211.

Footnotes are a convenience for the reader but a nuisance for the writer. Your chief difficulty is gauging how much space will be required. It is discouraging, to say the least, to finish typing a page neatly and correctly only to discover that there is no room for footnotes. Before you insert a sheet of paper in your typewriter, look through your rough draft to see how many notes will be needed and make a light pencil mark on the page where it will remind you to begin the footnotes. Be a little generous in your estimate because extra space looks better than crowded notes. Another method is to draw lines on a sheet of paper ten and fifteen spaces up from the bottom and then to use it as a backing sheet; the lines will show through and enable you to determine where the footnotes should begin.

Double-space twice between the text of your paper and the first footnote on the page. The extra space will separate the footnotes from the text. Single-space each footnote that runs two lines or more; double-space between footnotes. Do not write two footnotes, however short, on the same line. If a manuscript is to be printed, double-space each footnote and double-space between footnotes.

Footnotes may also be divided from the text by a line fifteen spaces long or by a continuous line across the page.

variant
variant

Primary Forms

When a source deviates from the standard primary form for a book or a magazine, use the checklist below to find a model to follow. The numbers of the examples correspond to the numbers identifying bibliographical examples, so that, when necessary, you can compare a note form with its bibliographical counterpart (pp. 108–22).

```
┌─────────────────────────────────────────────────────────────────────┐
│                   Checklist of Primary Note Forms                     │
│                                                                       │
│    Anonymous work 3   22,23,38      Multiple authorship 21            │
│    Anthology 4   32                 Newspaper 22                      │
│    Book, standard primary form 1    Pamphlet 23                       │
│    Collaborator 5                   Personal letter 24               │
│    Corporate author 6               Photocopy 25                      │
│    Edition 7   9                    Pseudonym 26                      │
│    Editor 8   4,28,32,33,36         Public document 27               │
│    Encyclopedia 9                   Published letter 28              │
│    Film 10                          Recording or cassette 29         │
│    Filmstrip 11                     Reprint 30                        │
│    Illustrator 12                   Review 31                         │
│    Interview 13                     Selection in anthology 32        │
│    Introduction 14   12             Series 33                         │
│    Joint authorship 15              Subtitle 34   14,36              │
│    Lecture 16                       Television or radio program 35   │
│    Legal reference 17               Title within a title 36   18     │
│    Magazine continuously paged 18   Translation 37                   │
│         2,28,36                     Untitled article 38              │
│    Magazine, standard primary form 2 Volume number 39               │
│    Manuscript materials 19               2,9,18,25,28,30,34,36       │
│    Microform 20                                                      │
└─────────────────────────────────────────────────────────────────────┘
```

A primary note is the first citation of a work. It should be complete enough to enable a reader to locate the work readily. The standard forms for books and magazines are illustrated here; primary forms for sources that deviate somehow from the basic form are shown on pages 126–35. Primary notes differ from bibliographic entries in the following ways:

Indentation is conventional (5 spaces).
Authors' names are not inverted.
Commas separate the items.
Publication facts for a book or for a magazine with a volume number are
enclosed in parentheses.
Exact page references are cited.

1. Book, Standard Primary Form _____

     ¹ Jessie Bernard, The Female World (New York, Free Press, 1981), p. 525.

variant   ¹ Jessie Bernard, The Female World (New York, 1981), p. 525.

Note that no comma is used before a parenthesis. If the publisher is named in the bibliography, the place and year of publication may be considered sufficient in a short paper. Citing the publisher is more common. Determine which form your instructor prefers and follow it consistently.

2. Magazine, Standard Primary Form

> [2] Bob Kuttner, "The Declining Middle," <u>Atlantic Monthly</u>, July 1983, p. 67.
>
> [3] Bernard Kiernan, "The Conservative Illusion," <u>Virginia Quarterly Review</u>, 59 (Spring 1983), 213.

In citing a magazine like *The Atlantic Monthly,* it is permissible to drop the initial "The." If you include the volume number for a magazine, enclose the issue date in parentheses. Arabic numerals are now in general use for volumes, but Roman *variant* numerals are acceptable if used consistently throughout a paper. If a volume number is cited, the page number is not preceded by the abbreviation "p."

Special Primary Forms

3. Anonymous Work

[4] <u>A Critical Fable</u> (Boston: Houghton Mifflin, 1922), p. 31.

[5] Anonymous, M.D., <u>The Healers</u> (New York: Putnam, 1967), p. 46.

[6] "Coping With Nature," <u>Time</u>, 29 Aug. 1983, p. 11.

Do not use the word "Anonymous" unless it appears on the title page of the book. If you want to identify the author of an anonymous work, it can be done most simply in the text of your paper.

4. Anthology

> [7] Sarah Blacker Cohen, ed., <u>From Hester Street to Hollywood</u> (Bloomington, Ind.: Indiana Univ. Press, 1983), p. 8.

Unless you quote from the commentary by an editor of an anthology, you would cite a specific selection rather than the entire book (see Example 32). The subtitle has been omitted from the above citation.

5. Collaborator

> [8] H. R. Haldeman, <u>The Ends of Power</u>, with Joseph DiMona (New York: Times Books, 1978), p. 101.

The name of a collaborator might be omitted since it appears in the bibliography.

6. Corporate Author

⁹ National Council of Teachers of English, Idea Exchange for English Teachers (Urbana, Ill.: NCTE, 1983), p. 16.

⁹ Idea Exchange for English Teachers, by National Council of Teachers of English (Urbana, Ill.: NCTE, 1983), p. 16.

When an organization or any other collective group is listed in the author-position on the title page of a book, it can be cited in either of the ways shown. The same order should be followed in both notes and bibliography.

7. Edition

¹⁰ Elmer Borklund, Contemporary Literary Criticism, 2nd ed. (Detroit: Gale, 1982), p. 47.

8. Editor

¹¹ William Saroyan, My Name Is Saroyan, ed. James H. Tashjian (New York: Coward-McCann, 1983), p. 103.

¹² Maria Roy, ed., The Abusive Partner (New York: Van Nostrand Reinhold, 1983), p. 206.

The original author of an edited work is cited in the author-position, and the editor's name follows the title. A subtitle has been omitted from the second example.

9. Encyclopedia

¹³ "Satire," Encyclopedia Americana, 1976 ed.

variant ¹³ Encyclopedia Americana, 1976 ed., s.v. "Satire."

variant ¹³ C. Hugh Holman, "Satire," Encyclopedia Americana, 1976 ed., vol. 24, p. 295.

The first form is the simplest way of citing an encyclopedia article. The abbreviation s.v. in the second example means sub verbo (under the word) and is often used to cite a portion of a work that is alphabetically arranged. The third example is unnecessarily cumbersome; the author, volume, and page are not needed to locate the article.

10. Film

¹⁴ Bruce Beresford, dir., Tender Mercies, prod. Philip S. Hobel, with Robert Duvall and Tess Harper, Universal Studios, 1983.

Since you are unlikely to quote from a film, you would cite it in a note only to identify some aspects of its production. Ordinarily the bibliography entry would be sufficient.

11. Filmstrip

¹⁵ Mythology Lives! (filmstrip), (Mount Kisco, N.Y.: Center for Humanities, 1983).

¹⁶ Joyce and Beckett (Princeton, N.J.: Films for the Humanities, 1983), (filmstrip FFH 353).

The medium can be designated immediately after the title or at the close.

12. Illustrator

¹⁷ Olaf Stapeldon, Nebula Maker & Four Encounters, introd. Arthur C. Clarke, illus. Jim Stalin (New York: Dodd, Mead, 1983), p. 42.

Unless the illustrations are discussed in the paper, the name of an illustrator can be omitted from a note.

13. Interview

¹⁸ Personal interview with Horace J. Bates, Memphis, Tenn., 18 Mar. 1984.

¹⁸ Personal interview, Memphis, Tenn., 18 Mar. 1984.

The second form would be sufficient if you identified your informant by name in the text of your paper.

14. Introduction

¹⁹ Monte Irvin, Introd., Invisible Men: Life in Baseball's Negro Leagues, by Donn Rogosin (New York: Athaneum, 1983), p. 6.

¹⁹ Donn Rogosin, Invisible Men: Life in Baseball's Negro Leagues, introd. Monte Irvin (New York: Athaneum, 1983), p. 143.

In the first example, the Introduction is quoted in the paper. Headings like Introduction or Preface are not enclosed in quotation marks and often are abbreviated. In the second example, the introduction is merely part of the description of the book and might be omitted from a note. The subtitle is included because it identifies the content of the book.

15. Joint Authorship

[20] John Chancellor and Walter R. Mears, The News Business (New York: Harper & Row, 1983), p. 47.

16. Lecture

[21] Mary W. Pickett, Public lecture, "The Rights of Minorities," Memphis, Tenn., 27 Oct. 1983.

Quote sparingly, if at all, from a lecture; it is usually better to summarize a speaker's ideas. The speaker, the title, the place, and the date are the basic facts.

17. Legal Reference

[22] 10 U. S. Code, Title 45, sec. d.

[23] U. S. Reports 824 (U.S. Sup. Ct. 1976).

[24] United States v. Marvin Mandel et al., 408 Federal Supplement 676 (U.S. Dist. Ct. Maryland 1976).

A split note (see H, pp. 137–38) is a useful means of simplifying a legal reference. In the first example, the law (Railroad Retirement Act of 1937) is identified in the text, and so the note includes only the volume and name of the source, the title number, and the section. A page number is not necessary. In the second example, the case has been named in the text of the paper; and so the note cites only the volume, name, and page of the law report, the court that heard the case, and the year in which it was decided. The third example includes the name of the case but is otherwise identical to the second. Publication data for legal references can be omitted from notes. A volume number precedes and page numbers follow the title of a volume. Names of laws or cases are not underlined or enclosed in quotation marks in documentation.

18. Magazine Continuously Paged

[25] Neil M. Flax, "The Presence of the Sign in Goethe's Faust," PMLA, 98 (1983), p. 197.

Because many scholarly journals are paginated continuously throughout a vol-

variant ume, only the year is necessary. Specifying the issue (Mar. 1983), however, would be very little trouble and would be a convenience to the reader.

19. Manuscript Materials

26 William Faulkner, Letter to Morton Goldman, 18 July 1935, Arents Coll., New York Library.

27 John Edwin Holsberry, Jr., "Hawthorne and the English Romantic Poets," Diss. Duke 1976, p. 73.

Manuscripts and other unpublished materials often require a degree of improvisation. There are often no page numbers. Follow the primary form for a book as closely as possible. Indicate the location of the manuscript. The title of a dissertation not published as a book is enclosed in quotation marks.

20. Microform

28 D. H. Mitchell, "Mushrooms," Mycology, No. 1 (Denver: Poisindex, 1974). Microfiche.

If you use a microform that is a reproduction of a printed source, cite the printed source. If the microform is the original source, identify the medium (microfiche) immediately after the title or at the end of the note.

21. Multiple Authorship

29 Erwin G. Krasnow, Lawrence D. Longley, and Herbert A. Terry, The Politics of Broadcast Regulation (New York: St. Martin's Press, 1982), p. 77.

30 Shafritz, Jay M., and others, Personnel Management in Government (New York: Marcel Dekker, 1978), p. 62.

Three authors are usually cited in a primary note. The second example is a book with four authors; only the first, followed by "and others," is necessary. The Latin
variant abbreviation "et al." might have been used, but it has been superseded by its English equivalent. A subtitle and the name of a series have been omitted from the second example; they would, of course, appear in the bibliography.

22. Newspaper

31 Evening Sun [Baltimore], 6 Oct. 1983, p. 17.

32 "Clean Air Costs," Editorial, Washington Post, 12 Aug. 1983, Sec. A, p. 16.

These examples cite a news story and an editorial. Except that commas replace periods, a note for a newspaper is the same as a bibliography entry (see Bibliography Example 22).

23. Pamphlet _____

[33] Why You Can Count on Cotton (Memphis, Tenn.: National Council, n.d.), p. 4.

Pamphlets often lack some publication data. Follow the normal order for a book entry and omit whatever is not available.

24. Personal Letter _____

[34] Letter received from Thomas Pynchon, 9 June 1984.

The word "received" might be omitted. If the writer of the letter was identified in the text, "Letter, 9 June 1984." would be sufficient.

25. Photocopy _____

[35] Merrill Maguire Skaggs, "Poe's Longing for a Bicameral Mind," Southern Quarterly, 19 (Winter 1981), p. 57. Photocopy.

Most photocopies that you will use will be reproductions of a printed article or book, and you can document them as you would the original. The word "photocopy," therefore, is not strictly necessary.

26. Pseudonym _____

[36] Petroleum V. Nasby, The Nasby Papers (Indianapolis: C. O. Perrine, 1864), p. 302.

If you wish to identify a pseudonym, do so in the text of your paper or in the bibliography (see Bibliography Example 26).

27. Public Document _____

[37] U.S.H.R. Committee on Ways and Means, Caribbean Basin Initiative, 97th Cong., 2nd sess., p. 76.

[38] Cong. Rec. (Daily), 15 Sept. 1983, p. S12314.

Note forms for public documents should be kept as simple as possible. Publication facts can be omitted. Compare these forms with Bibliography Example 27. The split note (see **H**, pp. 137–38) is especially useful. Such facts as the name of a witness or the date of a hearing can be given in the text and need not be repeated in a note. The second example refers to remarks by Senator Charles Percy, who could be identified in the text.

28. Published Letter _____

[39] P. T. Barnum to Samuel L. Clemens, 10 Oct. 1877, Selected Letters of P. T. Barnum, ed. A. H. Saxon (New York: Columbia Univ. Press, 1983), p. 202.

variant   [39] PTB to Samuel L. Clemens, 10 Oct. 1877, A. H. Saxon, ed., Selected Letters of P. T. Barnum (New York: Columbia Univ. Press, 1983), p. 202.

[40] Ellsworth Barnard, Letter, "The Language of Criticism," PMLA, 98 (1983), p. 87.

The citation of a letter should identify the writer, the recipient, and the date. If several letters by the same writer are used and if there is no possibility of confusion, the writer can be identified by initials, as in the second example. The second example also shows an alternative postition for the editor's name. The third example is a letter to the editor; its title was assigned by the journal that printed it.

29. Recording or Cassette _____

[41] Harry Halbreich, Jacket Notes, Symphony No. 1 in D Major, by Gustav Mahler, cond. Erich Leinsdorf, Royal Philharmonic Orchestra, London Records, SMAS 94801, 1972.

[41] Gustav Mahler, Symphony No. 1 in D Major, cond. Erich Leinsdorf, Royal Philharmonic Orchestra, London Record, SMAS 94801, 1972.

[42] Dropping Out: Road to Nowhere, Center for Humanities, Video cassette V-6793-3070, 1983.

You would use the first form if you quoted from the commentary on the liner of a record album. The second and third examples simply identify a recording and a cassette. Since there is no way of specifying a particular portion of a recording and usually no necessity for doing so and since recordings would be listed in the bibliography, a citation note seems unnecessary. Note that the title of a musical composition that merely identifies its form, number, and key is not underlined.

30. Reprint _____

[43] Barrett Wendell, A Literary History of America (1900; rpt. New York: Haskell House, 1968), p. 87.

[44] Henry Mayhew, London Labour and the London Poor (London, 1862; rpt. New York: Dover, 1968), vol. 4, p. 103.

In a short paper, it may be unnecessary to include this information in a note since it appears in the bibliography. The citation in the second example might be written IV, 103, but this would commit the writer to consistent use of Roman numerals for volumes.

31. Review

[45] Rev. of <u>Pandora's Box</u>, <u>New Yorker</u>, 19 Sept. 1983, p. 30.

[46] Arthur M. Schlesinger, Jr., "Requiem for Neoliberalism," rev. of <u>A New Democracy</u>, by Gary Hart, <u>New Republic</u>, 6 June 1963, p. 29.

The examples above illustrate an unsigned, untitled review and a signed review with a title. The abbreviation "Rev." should be written out if there is any chance of its being confused with "Revision."

32. Selection in Anthology

[47] Enoch Brater, "Ethnics and Ethnicity in the Plays of Arthur Miller," in <u>From Hester Street to Hollywood</u>, ed. Sarah Blacker Cohen (Bloomington, Ind.: Indiana Univ. Press, 1983), p. 127.

The author or the title of the selection or both might be identified in the text and thus shorten the note (see discussion of Split Note, **H,** p. 138). The subtitle of the anthology has been omitted above.

33. Series

[48] John Matzer, Jr., ed., <u>Capital Financing Strategies for Local Governments</u>, Practical Management Series (Washington, D.C.: International City Management Assn., 1983), p. 127.

[48] John Matzer, Jr., ed., <u>Capital Financing Strategies for Local Governments</u> (Washington, D.C.: International City Management Assn.), p. 127.

Because a series will be cited in the bibliography, it can be omitted from a note. The second form above, therefore, seems preferable.

34. Subtitle

[49] Helen Benedict, "Bernard Malamud: Morals and Surprises," <u>Antioch Review</u>, 41 (Winter 1983), 31.

[49] Helen Benedict, "Bernard Malamud," <u>Antioch Review</u>, 41 (Winter 1983), 31.

A subtitle, like the name of a series, can usually be omitted from a primary note. In rare instances it may be needed to identify the content of a work.

35. Television or Radio Program _____

50 Arthur C. Clarke's Mysterious World, PBS TV, 20 Oct. 1983.

Since you cannot cite a specific portion of a program and the content is not retrievable by a reader, you should identify the program in the text and list it in the bibliography. A note is seldom necessary.

36. Title within a Title _____

51 Ellin Ringer, "Middlemarch: A Feminist Perspective," Studies in the Novel, 15 (Spring 1983), p. 58.

52 Lisa Ruddick, "'Melanctha' and the Psychology of William James," Modern Fiction Studies, 28 (Winter 1982-83), p. 551.

53 "The American Scholar" Today, ed. C. David Mead (New York: Dodd, Mead, 1970), p. 27.

54 Oscar Mandel, Annotations to Vanity Fair (Washington, D.C.: University Press of America, 1981), p. 34.

The possible combinations in which one title can appear within another title are the same in notes as in bibliographies (see Bibliography Example 36). The subtitle has been retained in the first example because it identifies the content of the article; the subtitle in the third example has been omitted.

37. Translation _____

55 Simone de Beauvoir, When Things of the Spirit Come First, trans. Patrick O'Brien (New York: Pantheon, 1982), p. 42.

The name of the translator would come first only if the translation itself was the main concern of the paper.

38. Untitled Article _____

56 Time, 19 Sept. 1983, p. 82.

[57] Joseph Blotner, _Faulkner_ (New York: Random House, 1974), vol. 2, p. 56.

[58] Leon Edel, _The Treacherous Years_, Vol. 4 of _Henry James_ (Philadelphia: Lippincott, 1969), pp. 58-60.

variant The subtitle "A Biography" has been omitted from the first example, and "1895–1901" has been omitted from the second. Roman numerals (II, 56 and Vol. IV) might be used instead of Arabic.

Secondary Forms

It is a basic principle of documentation that a primary note should contain all the information needed to identify and locate a source and that subsequent citations (secondary forms) should be as concise as posible. If you have a problem involving a secondary note, consult the checklist below to find the relevant explanation and illustrative examples.

Checklist of Secondary Forms

Abbreviated title **F**   _Ibid._ **B**
Consecutive citations **A**   Internal citation **E**
Divided works **G**   Nonconsecutive citations **C**
Double reference **J**   _op.cit._ **D**
Graphic materials **I**   Split note **H**

A   Consecutive Citations

[1] Bernard, p. 270.

[1] p. 270.

variant   [1] _Ibid._, p. 270.

B When a note refers to the same source as the immediately preceding reference, either the author and the page number or the page number alone is sufficient. _Ibid._ (in the same place) can also be used in this situation, but like other Latin abbreviations, _Ibid._ is used less often than formerly. Consecutive citations are often justified, but several such sequences may indicate that you are following one source too closely.

C Nonconsecutive Citations

— abb title of artical

[2] Bernard, p. 270.

[2] Bernard, Female World, p. 270.

variant [2] Bernard, op. cit., p. 270.

[3] Kuttner, p. 67.

[3] Kuttner, "Illusion," p. 67.

[3] Kuttner, Virginia Quarterly Review, p. 67.

variant [3] Kuttner, op. cit., p. 67.

Most secondary notes are in this category. The author's last name may be sufficient; but if you have two authors with the same last names, you must include their first names or initials, and the result may still be confusing. If you use two books by the same author, you should include a short form of the title for each. To avoid confusion, it may be prudent to use short titles consistently. Either the name of a magazine or a shortened title of an article is acceptable; the latter is somewhat more convenient for a reader.

D

variant Instead of a short title, the abbreviation *op. cit.* (work previously cited) can be used, but its reference can be maddeningly elusive if it appears several pages after the primary citation, and it cannot be used if you have two or more books by the same author. It is always used with the author's name. Like *Ibid.,* this abbreviation is rapidly becoming obsolete.

E Internal Citation

[4] Jessie Bernard, The Female World (New York: Free Press, 1981), p. 86; hereafter cited within the text.

Women find it difficult to assume a meaningful role in society because they are "trained to be nonassertive, compliant, agreeable, to serve others" (Bernard, p. 525).

Throughout the 19th century, according to Jessie Bernard, many objected to women working for a living because it was feared that they would lose their feminine nature (pp. 523-25).

When a work is cited several times in a paper, citations can be made parenthetically within the text. This economical and sensible procedure is relatively new, but its use is increasing. The first reference should be a primary note followed by a brief indication that further citations will be made within the text. In this example, the semicolon and the position of the phrase are standard, but other language such as "subsequent references in the text" could be used. The two examples above illustrate the basic procedure: The citation is enclosed in parentheses, it follows quotation marks, and it precedes any punctuation of your own. If the author is clearly identified elsewhere, the page number is sufficient. As the second example shows, internal citation can be used for a summary as well as for a quotation.

F Abbreviated Title

⁵ Philip José Farmer, <u>Gods of Riverworld</u> (New York: Putnam, 1983), p. 42; hereafter cited as <u>GOR</u> within the text.

A technique that can be used in conjunction with internal citation is the abbreviation of a title. This procedure is especially useful in a paper dealing with one or more literary works, but it should not be overused. A half-dozen abbreviated titles in a short paper could create confusion.

The Bible is usually cited internally. The titles of Biblical books are not underlined, and longer ones can be abbreviated. The order in the first example below is Book, Chapter, Verses, separated by unspaced periods. The same punctuation is used for plays divided into acts, scenes, and lines and for long poems divided into books or cantos, stanzas, and lines. The second example below is a citation of Shakespeare's *Love's Labour's Lost,* and the third cites Spenser's *The Faerie Queene.*

G

(I Chron.xvii.19-21)

(LLL V.i.16-18)

(FQ I.xi.118-19)

H Split Note

⁶ <u>Neill of Summerhill: The Permanent Rebel</u> (New York: Pantheon, 1983), <u>p. 390.</u>

⁷ p. 126.

Another time-saving device is the split note, which is based on the principle that information appearing in the text of a paper ordinarily need not be repeated in a note. The first example is a primary note for a book identified by author and title in the paper. The title is repeated even though it appears in the text; the subtitle, however, might have been omitted. The second example is a secondary citation of a work clearly identified in the text of the paper. Actually a reference like this could be made just as easily within the paper (see discussion of Internal Citation, **E**). In some circumstances, however, split notes are the most efficient means of documentation.

I   Graphic Materials

Reproduced from Robert E. Riegel, America Moves West, rev. ed. (New York: Holt, 1974), p. 75.

Because it is often difficult to place the reference number where it will be noticed, a map, graph, diagram, or chart ordinarily should be cited in a credit line directly beneath the borrowed material rather than in a footnote. The credit line is not numbered.

J   Double Reference

[8] Joseph Freeman, An American Testament, quoted in Arthur Mizener, The Far Side of Paradise (Boston: Houghton Mifflin, 1951), p. 111.

[8] Arthur Mizener, The Far Side of Paradise (Boston: Houghton Mifflin, 1951), p. 111, quoting Joseph Freeman, An American Testament, p. 246.

A problem that seems to arise more often in classroom discussions of research papers than in actual writing situations is the citation of a source that is quoted in the work you are using. Both notes above are correct but somewhat cumbersome. There are two ways of avoiding this kind of awkward indirect reference. You can name either your source or the original source in the text of your paper (see discussion of Split Note, **H**). It is also legitimate to find the original source and use it; it may include other material relevant to your topic.

STYLES IN OTHER DISCIPLINES

Different minds have different perplexities.

In most courses in the Natural and Social Sciences, you will need to use and interpret forms and procedures of documentation very different from the conventional Humanities style. Every scholarly journal has its own style requirements, and there is no academic field in which procedures are completely uniform. An authoritative guide that is not restricted to a particular discipline is *The Chicago Manual of Style,* 13th ed. (Chicago: Univ. of Chicago, 1982); but it is intended for professional authors, editors, and book designers and is, therefore, too technical for most student writing.

Some general procedures are described below, and typical documentation in nine academic disciplines is described briefly and illustrated.

LISTING SOURCES

The sources used in a paper are usually listed at the close under a heading like "References" or "Works Cited." They may be arranged in alphabetical order or in the order in which they are referred to in the paper. If you have a choice of methods, list them alphabetically.

Authors' given names are often reduced to initials. There is considerable variation in the form of titles. Generally only the first word of a title is capitalized ("down style"), the title of an article is not enclosed in quotation marks, and the title of a book or a journal is not underlined. Names of journals more than one word long are often abbreviated. The form of a reference resembles the *Readers' Guide* system (18:134–42); the number on the left of the colon identifies the volume, and numbers on the right indicate pages. A volume number is sometimes printed in boldface type (indicated in a manuscript by a wavy line under the number).

In fields where the recency of research is especially significant, the year of publication is emphasized by placing it immediately after the author's name or at the very end of an entry. In an alphabetical listing, if an author has published two or more works in the same year, each is assigned a letter: 1984a, 1984b.

CITATION

Internal citation (see **E,** pp. 136–37) is the basis of most systems. Especially in the Natural Sciences, entire works rather than specific pages are usually cited. Direct quotation is used sparingly. The two methods of citation in general use are the *author–year system* and the *number system.*

Author–Year Citation

The author–year system, which is in general use, is less confusing for a reader. If the author is identified in the sentence, only the year of publication is cited in parentheses:

```
It has been demonstrated by Tukey (1977) that . . .
```

Otherwise, both author and year are cited:

```
Analysis of data (Tukey 1977) indicates . . .
```

Page references are included when appropriate:

```
A statistical table (Tukey, 1977, p. 48) suggests . . .
```

Number Citation

In the number system, sources in the list of references are numbered beginning with 1. The numeral is sometimes written as a superscript. Citation is accomplished within the text by inserting the number of the source above the line or within parentheses. Multiple citation is common:

```
Recent research 2, 6, 8 suggests . . .
```

```
Recent research (2-6-8) suggests . . .
```

A page reference can be included in a reference:

```
Analysis of partially ionized gases (7, p. 183) has . . .
```

The number system can be confusing and also requires a reader to consult constantly the list of references to identify the source represented by a number.

Biology

Keddy, P. A., and A. A. Reznicek. 1981. The role of reed banks in the persistence of Ontario's coastal plain flora. American Journal of Botany 69: 13-22.

Hartwell, L. H. & Ungar, M. W. (1977). J. cell Biol. 75, 422.

Tukey, J. W. 1977. Exploratory data analysis. Addison-Wesley, Reading, Massachusetts.

Martin, Y. C. (1978). Quantitative Drug Design. New York: Marcel Dekker.

The examples above illustrate the extremes of variation. In the first example, the title and the name of the journal are written in full and there are inclusive page references. In the second example, the title of the article is omitted, and only the first page is cited. The listings for books, the third and fourth examples, differ chiefly in arrangement and in minor matters such as the enclosure of the year in parentheses. See Council of Biology Editors, Committee on Form and Style, *CBE Style Manual,* 4th ed. (Washington, D.C.: American Inst. of Biological Sciences, 1978).

Chemistry

(9) Cooks, R. G. "Collision Spectroscopy"; Plenum Press: New York, 1978.

(10) Freas, R. D.; Ridge, D. P. J. Am. Chem. Soc. 1980, 102, 7129.

(11) Jacobson, D. B.; Freiser, B. J. J. Am. Chem. Soc. 1983, 105, 736.

There are more minor variations in Chemistry than in most fields. These *foot-notes* from the *Journal of the American Chemical Society* are representative. Book titles are enclosed in quotation marks. Articles are not identified by title, and only the first page is cited. Some journals use the number system of citation but place explanation notes at the bottom of the page. See American Chemical Society, *Handbook for Authors of Papers in the Journals of the American Chemical Society* (Washington, D.C.: American Chemical Society, 1978).

Economics

Bettman, James, An Information Processing Theory of Consumer Choice. Addison-Wesley, Reading, Mass., 1979.

Radolf, Andrew, "Knight-Kidder to Test Home Electronic Info System," Editor and Publisher, April 12, 1980, pp. 7-8.

Wright, Peter, and Peter Rip, "Product Class Advertising Effects on First-Time Buyers' Decision Strategies," Journal of Consumer Research, 1980, Vol. 7 (2), pp. 176-188.

Usage varies but is basically conservative with relatively few abbreviations or other shortcuts. The publisher of a book precedes the place and the year. The author–year system of citation predominates, but some journals use the number system. Explanation notes are placed at the bottom of the page. See Conrad Berenson and Raymond Colton, *Research and Report Writing for Business and Economics* (New York: Random House, 1971).

Education

Bakalis, Michael J. (1981) American education and the meaning of scarcity, Phi Delta Kappan, pt. 1, 63, pp. 7-12, September, and pt. 2, 63, pp. 102-105, October.

Burton, Nancy W. & Jones, Lyle V. (1982) Recent trends in achievement levels of black and white youth, Educational Researcher, 11, pp. 10-14, April.

Carnegie Council on Policy Studies in Higher Education (1979) Giving Youth a Better Chance: options for education, work and service (San Francisco, Jossey-Bass).

Freeman, Roger A. (1981) The Wayward Welfare State (Stanford, Hoover Institute Press).

Usage varies widely. Some journals follow APA style. Titles of articles are sometimes enclosed in quotation marks and capitalized but are sometimes written like the first two examples above. The month is placed at the close of a magazine citation. The place of publication and the publisher of books are cited in parentheses. Both the author–year and the number systems are used, and some journals use footnotes. See National Education Assn., *NEA Style Manual for Writers and Editors,* rev. ed. (Washington, D.C.: National Education Assn., 1974).

History

Rose, Anne C. Transcendentalism as a Social Movement, 1830-1850. New Haven: Yale University Press, 1981.

Numbers, Ronald L. and Janet S. Numbers. "Science in the Old South: A Reappraisal." The Journal of Southern History, 48 (May 1982), 163-184.

[1] Anne C. Rose, Transcendentalism as a Social Movement, 1830-1850 (New Haven, 1981): p. 106.

[2] Ronald L. Numbers and Janet S. Numbers, "Science in the Old South: A Reappraisal," The Journal of Southern History 48 (May 1982): p. 176.

Documentation in History resembles conventional Humanities style. The first two examples are bibliography entries; the last two are primary notes. The chief differences are the omission of publishers from notes and the use of a colon before a page citation. Footnotes are more common than endnotes. See Jacques Barzun and Henry F. Graff, *The Modern Researcher,* 3rd ed. (New York: Harcourt Brace, 1977).

Physics

[1] G. F. Knoll, <u>Radiation Detection and Measurement</u> (Wiley, New York, 1979), pp. 414-466.

[2] Kyle Griggs, Science 1981, 842 (1973).

[3] W. R. French, Jr., R. L. LaShure, and J. L. Curran, Am. J. Phys. 37, 11 (1969).

Documentation in Physics is more uniform than in most fields; it is also more divergent from conventional Humanities style. Titles of books are underlined, but names of journals are not. Titles of articles are not shown. Superscript numerals are used to identify sources. Only the first page of an article is cited. References may be placed at the bottom of each page or in a terminal list. See American Institute of Physics, Publications Board, *Style Manual for Guidance in the Preparation of Papers,* 3rd rev. ed. (New York: American Institute of Physics, 1978).

Political Science

Andur, R. Rawls and his radical critics, <u>Dissent</u>, 1980, 27, 323-334.

Dahl, R. <u>Dilemmas of a pluralist democracy</u>. New Haven, Conn.: Yale University Press, 1982.

Thomas, H., & Logan, C. <u>Mondragon: an economic analysis</u>. London: Allen & Unwin, 1982.

In general, style in Political Science is similar to that used in Psychology except that the year is not placed after an author's name. Only the first word of a title is capitalized. The author–year system is most commonly used, but explanation notes are placed at the bottom of the page.

Psychology

Anderson, J. R. (1983). <u>The architecture of cognition</u>. Cambridge: Harvard Univ. Press.

Becker, C. A. (1980). Semantic context effects in visual word recognition: An analysis of semantic strategies. <u>Memory and Cognition, 8</u> 493-512.

Frazier, L. & Fodor, J. D. (1978). The sausage machine: A new two-stage parsing model. <u>Cognition,</u> 6 291-325.

Standard forms are shown above. Only the first word of a title or of a subtitle is capitalized. Volume numbers are underlined or marked for boldface type (a wavy line). All authors are named unless there are more than six, in which case *et al.* is used with the first name. Author–year citation is most common, but the number system is sometimes used. See American Psychological Assn., *Publication Manual of the American Psychological Association,* 2nd rev. ed. (Washington, D.C.: American Psychological Assn., 1983).

Sociology _____

Elder, Glen H., Jr.

    1974 Children of the Great Depression. Chicago: University of Chicago Press.

    1978 "Approaches to social change and the family." American Journal of Sociology 84:1-38.

Eysenick, H. J. and James A Wakefield

    1981 "Psychological factors as predictors of marital satisfaction." Advances in Behavior Research and Therapy 3: 151-91.

Scharf, Lois

    1980 To Work and to Wed: Female Employment, Feminism, and the Great Depression. Westport, CT: Greenwood Press.

Some journals in Sociology follow the sensible and convenient practice of placing an author's name by itself on the first line. Two or more works by the same author are arranged chronologically. Only the first word in the title of an article is capitalized, and quotation marks are used; the title of a book is capitalized conventionally but is not underlined. There is no punctuation after the name of a journal. The *Readers' Guide* system is used for volume and pages. Postal abbreviations are used for states. The most common form of citation is author–year. Basic conventions are summarized in each issue of *American Sociological Review.*

NEW MLA STYLE

Of composition there are different methods.

The second edition of *MLA Handbook for Writers of Research Papers* (1984) describes a style of documentation considerably different from the conventional style used in the Humanities heretofore. In some respects it resembles the styles in other disciplines discussed in the last section, but it is simpler and more consistent than most of them.

Anyone inclined to write a facetious account of new scholarly procedures in the Humanities might consider the following titles:

"The Vanishing Footnote"
"The Decline and Fall of the Roman Numeral"
"Where Have All the Ibids Gone?"

As these imaginary titles may suggest, the basic purpose of the changes has been simplification. They are based on the recognition that documentation is a means, not an end; it is simply apparatus intended to enable a reader to retrieve or verify information as readily as possible.

The new style is not a sudden change but the culmination of a number of general trends discussed earlier in this chapter: the increased use of endnotes rather than footnotes, the use of split notes and internal citation, the replacement of Roman numerals by Arabic, and the decreased use of Latin abbreviations. The purpose underlying all such changes has been to make documentation more functional and more efficient.

The basic procedure of the new style is very simple: all research materials are listed alphabetically at the end of a paper, and borrowed materials are cited briefly within the text, usually by the author's last name and the page reference: (Bernard 525-26). Citation notes, therefore, either as footnotes or as endnotes, are unnecessary. Explanation notes, if any are needed, are numbered as in conventional documentation and written on a page headed "Notes," a separate sheet just before the list of works cited. Brief reference notes can be cited internally; longer ones can be assigned numbers and included on the note page. In a paper requiring no explanation or reference notes, all citation would be internal.

LISTING SOURCES AS WORKS CITED

All sources, print and nonprint, that contribute facts or opinions, whether quoted or paraphrased, are listed at the close of a paper. The list is alphabetical. It is headed "Works Cited."

The citation of books differs only slightly from the conventional bibliographical forms described on pages 108–22.

1. Book, Standard Form _____

Bernard, Jessie. The Female World. New York: Free, 1981.

Brownell, W.C. French Traits: An Essay in Comparative Criticism. New

York, 1896.

The major difference in the standard form is that publishers' names are shortened drastically. The word "Press" is omitted, a compound name is reduced to the first element (Houghton instead of Houghton Mifflin), and University Press is shortened to UP. Other minor differences are illustrated in subsequent examples.

As the second example indicates, a publisher is not cited for a work published before 1900.

2. Magazine, Standard Forms _____

Drew, Elizabeth. "A Political Journal." New Yorker 26 Sept. 1983: 140-49.

Kuttner, Bob. "The Declining Middle." Atlantic Monthly July 1983: 60-72.

Somtow, S.P. "Galactic Garbage Art." Fantasy Review April 1984: 10+.

Kiernan, Bernard. "The Conservative Illusion." Virginia Quarterly

Review 59 (1983): 208-22.

Tapscott, Stephen. "Pandemonium in Xanadu." Romanticism Past and

Present 5.2 (1981): 23-40.

Most of the innovations in form occur in the publication facts that follow the name of the periodical. Major ones are summarized below.

1. No punctuation follows the name of the periodical.
2. A weekly or monthly magazine is identified by its date rather than by a volume number. The date is followed by a colon, a space, and inclusive page numbers.
3. The abbreviations p. and pp. are not used; numbers on the right of a colon are assumed to represent pagination.
4. If an article is not printed on consecutive pages, the first page is cited followed by a plus sign with no space between to indicate continuation in subsequent pages of the same issue.
5. A quarterly is identified by its volume number. Arabic numerals are used for volumes, and the abbreviation vol. is not used.
6. For a quarterly that is paged continuously throughout a volume, the year of

publication in parentheses follows the volume number. A colon, a space, and inclusive page numbers follow the year.

7. For a quarterly paged separately in each issue, the number of the issue follows the volume number. They are separated by a period. The year is cited in parentheses, followed by a colon, a space, and inclusive page numbers.

The sources illustrated as bibliography entries on pages 108–22 appear below in new MLA style. They are assigned the same reference numbers so that the boxed index on page 108 can be used to identify an example and two versions of the same citation can readily be compared. A few additional examples have been included to illustrate special problems. Most examples are self-explanatory, but brief comments are included when appropriate. At the close of this section in a miscellaneous category, there are also examples of the following special sources:

a cartoon
computer software
a map
a musical score
a performance
a work of art

3. Anonymous Works _____

A Critical Fable. Boston: Houghton, 1922.

Anonymous, M.D. The Healers. New York: Putnam, 1967.

"Coping with Nature." Time 29 Aug. 1983: 10-11.

4. Anthology _____

Cohen, Sara Blacker, ed. From Hester Street to Hollywood: The Jewish-
American Stage and Screen. Bloomington: Indiana UP, 1983.

5. Collaborator _____

Haldeman, H.R. The Ends of Power. With Joseph DiMona. New York: Times
Books, 1978.

Hoffa, James R. Hoffa: The Real Story. As Told to Oscar Fraley. New
York: Stein and Day, 1975.

6. Corporate Author _____

National Council of Teachers of English. <u>Idea Exchange for English</u>

   <u>Teachers</u>. Urbana: NCTE, 1983.

   A book is cited by its corporate author even though the same group is the publisher. As this example and others show, states are identified less often in new MLA
style.

7. Edition _____

Borklund, Elmer. <u>Contemporary Literary Criticism</u>. 2nd ed. Detroit:

   Gale, 1982.

Ellman, Richard. <u>James Joyce</u>. Rev. ed. New York: Oxford UP, 1982.

8. Editor _____

Saroyan, William. <u>My Name Is Saroyan</u>. Ed. James H. Tashjian. New York:

   Coward, 1983.

Roy, Maria, ed. <u>The Abusive Partner: An Analysis of Domestic Battery</u>.

   New York: Van Nostrand, 1983.

9. Encyclopedia _____

Holman, C. Hugh. "Satire." <u>Encyclopedia Americana</u>. 1976 ed.

"Luddites." <u>Encyclopaedia Britannica: Micropaedia</u>. 1974 ed.

   MLA recommends giving the author's name first for a signed article and the title
first for an unsigned article. Volume and page numbers are omitted for a reference
work that is alphabetically arranged. A publisher is not cited for a standard reference
work.

10. Film _____

<u>Tender Mercies</u>. Dir. Bruce Beresford. Prod. Philip S. Hobel. With Robert

   Duvall and Tess Harper. Universal Studios, 1983.

   The standard citation for a film is shown above, but if your paper is concerned with the work of one person (for example, the director, producer, screen writer, or performer), begin with that person's name.

11. Filmstrip _____

Mythology Lives! Filmstrip. Mount Kisco, NY: Center for Humanities, 1983.

The medium, capitalized but not underlined or quoted, follows the title. Bibliographical information follows as closely as possible the form for a book.

12. Illustrator _____

Stapledon, Olaf. Nebular Maker & Four Encounters. Introd. Arthur C.

Clark. Illus. Jim Stalin. New York: Dodd, Mead, 1983.

13. Interview _____

Bates, Horace J. Personal interview. Memphis, 18 Mar. 1984.

Fuller, Mary. Telephone interview. 12 Jan. 1984.

A published interview conducted by someone else is cited like an article in a journal or a newspaper. The word "Interview," not quoted or underlined, follows the title.

14. Introduction _____

Irvin, Monte. Introduction. Invisible Men: Life in Baseball's Negro

Leagues. By Donn Rogosin. New York: Antheneum, 1983.

The same form is followed for a preface, a foreword, or an afterword. The designation for the part being cited is capitalized but is not quoted or underlined.

15. Joint Authorship _____

Chancellor, John, and Walter R. Mears. The News Business. New York:

Harper, 1983.

Weisberg, Herbert I., and Thomas J. Tomberlin. "Statistical Evidence in

Employment Discrimination Cases." Statistical Methods & Reseach

11 (1983): 381-406.

16. Lecture _____

Pickett, Mary W. Public lecture, "The Rights of Minorities." Memphis,

    27 Oct. 1983.

Murphy, George. Class lecture. Sociology 402, Westminister College,

    17 Jan. 1984.

17. Legal Reference _____

10 US Code. Title 45, Secs. 228a-228z. 1971.

US Const. Art. 2, sec. 4.

Brown v. General Services Administration et al. 425 US Reports 820-39.

    No. 74-768. US Sup. Ct. 1976.

    The citation of legal documents and law cases should be simplified as much as possible. For special problems, consult the most recent edition of *A Uniform System of Citations,* published by Harvard Law Review Association. The United States Code, often abbreviated US Code or USC, is not underlined; it is preceded by the title number but is alphabetized under "U." Works like this are cited by sections with the year added if relevant.

    The name of a law case is underlined in the text but not in a citation. The general order is the parties to the case, the volume, title, and pages of the report, the number of the case, the court that decided the case, and the year of the decision.

18. Magazine Continuously Paged _____

Flax, Neil M. "The Presence of the Sign in Goethe's Faust." PMLA 98

    (1983): 183-203.

19. Manuscript Materials _____

Faulkner, William. Letter to Morton Goldman. 18 July 1935. Arents

    Coll. New York Public Library.

Melville, Herman. Journal for August 1860. Papers and Library of the

    Melville Family. Harvard Library.

Worthie, Peleg. Diary 1862-65. (Two manuscript notebooks owned by the
Worthie Family, Newton, Ohio.)

Holsberry, John Edwin, Jr. "Hawthorne and the English Romantic Poets."
Diss. Duke, 1976.

20. Microform

Mitchell, D. H. "Mushrooms," Microfiche. Mycology, no. 1. Denver:
Poisindex, 1974.

Identify the medium immediately after the title.

21. Multiple Authorship

Krasnow, Erwin G., Lawrence D. Longley, and Herbert A. Terry. The
Politics of Broadcast Regulation. New York: St. Martin's, 1982.

Shafritz, Jay M., et al. Personnel Management in Government: Politics
and Process. Publications in Public Policy. New York: Dekker, 1978.

If the work has three authors or editors, all three are cited. If there are more than
three, MLA favors the Latin abbreviation et al. (and others).

22. Newspaper

Evening Sun [Baltimore] 2-7 Oct. 1983.

"Senators Disclose Arms Limit Proposal." Atlanta Constitution 12 Sept.
1983: A2.

"Clean Air Costs." Editorial. Washington Post 12 Aug. 1983: A16.

Baker, Russell. "This Garrulous Silence." New York Times 14 Sept. 1983,
late ed.: 23.

If you designate a particular edition, follow the form of the fourth example
above.

23. Pamphlet

Dickman, Irving R. Behavior Modification. New York: Public Affairs
    Comm., 1976.

Dittrich, Kathinka, and Henry Marx, eds. Cultural Guide for Berlin.
    n.p.: n.p., n.d.

Why You Can Count on Cotton. Memphis: National Cotton Council, n.d.

Eating for Better Health. Washington, DC: GPO, 1981.

24. Personal Letter

Pynchon, Thomas. Personal letter. 9 June 1984.

25. Photocopy

Skaggs, Merrill Maguire. "Poe's Longing for a Bicameral Mind." Southern
    Quarterly 19.2 (1981): 54-64. Photocopy.

   If you use some type of photographic reproduction of a source, cite it as you
would the original and designate the medium at the close of the entry.

26. Pseudonym

Nasby, Petroleum V. [David Ross Locke]. The Nasby Papers. Indianapolis,
    1864.

27. Public Document

United States H.R. "Panama Canal Authorization, Fiscal Year 1982."
    Report No. 97-64. In House Reports, Nos. 59-90. 97th Cong. 1st
    sess. Washington, DC: GPO, 1981.

United States H.R. Committee on Ways and Means. Caribbean Basin
    Initiative. 97th Cong., 2nd sess. Washington, DC: GPO, 1982.

United States Office of Management and Budget. <u>Budget</u> <u>of</u> <u>the</u> <u>United</u>

 <u>States</u> <u>Government</u>, <u>Fiscal</u> <u>Year</u> <u>1983</u>. Washington, DC: GPO, 1983.

Coral Gables, FL. <u>Annual</u> <u>Financial</u> <u>Report</u>. Coral Gables, FL: Finance

 Dept., 1980.

<u>Cong</u>. <u>Rec</u>. 15 Sept. 1983: S12313-14.

  Public documents are so varied that some improvisation is often necessary. In general, you cite the name of the government, the agency, the title of the document and whatever information is needed to identify it. The publication facts can usually be cited like a book. The new MLA style uses postal abbreviations (see p. 166).

28. Published Letter

Saxon, A. H., ed. <u>Selected</u> <u>Letters</u> <u>of</u> <u>P.T.Barnum</u>. New York: Columbia

 UP, 1983.

Barnard, Ellsworth. Letter. "The Language of Criticism." <u>PMLA</u>, 98

 (1983): 87.

29. Recording or Cassette

Mahler, Gustav. Symphony No. 1 in D Major. Cond. Erich Leinsdorf. Royal

 Philharmonic Orchestra. London Records, SMAS 94801, 1972.

Halbreich, Harry. Jacket Notes. Symphony No. 1 in D Major. Cond. Erich

 Leinsdorf, Royal Philharmonic Orchestra. London Records, SMAS

 94801, 1972.

Eliot, T.S. "The Wasteland." <u>Caedmon</u> <u>Treasury</u> <u>of</u> <u>Modern</u> <u>Poets</u>. Caedmon,

 TC2006A, n.d.

<u>Dropping</u> <u>Out</u>: <u>Road</u> <u>to</u> <u>Nowhere</u>. Videocassette Center for Humanities,

 V-6793-3070, 1983.

  The citation of a recording can begin with the composer, the conductor, or the performer, depending on the emphasis in your paper. Major elements in the citation are separated by periods. The manufacturer and the number are followed by commas. If jacket notes or some other form of commentary is used in the paper, cite it first and follow it with information on the recording. Terms like "Jacket Notes," "Videocassette," or "Audiotape" are not underlined or quoted.

30. Reprint

Wendell, Barrett. A Literary History of America. 1900. New York:

    Haskell, 1968.

Mayhew, Henry. London Labour and the London Poor. 4 vols. London,

    1861-62. New York: Dover, 1968.

Bailey, J.O. Pilgrims through Space and Time. 1947. Westport, CT:

    Greenwood, 1972.

Malamud, Bernard. The Natural. 1952. New York: Dell, 1965.

    To cite a reprint, give the date of the original edition after the title. Follow it with publication data for the edition you are using. For a work first published outside the United States, include the city with the date of publication if possible.

31. Review

Rev. of Pandora's Box. New Yorker 19 Sept. 1983: 30.

D. O. Rev. of The Oxford Book of Death, ed. D. J. Enright. Harper's

    Aug. 1983: 75.

Schlesinger, Arthur M. Jr. "Requiem for Neoliberalism." Rev. of A New

    Democracy, by Gary Hart. New Republic 6 June 1983: 28-30.

Crist, Judith. "Bergman's Rosetta Stone." Rev. of Fanny and Alexander.

    Saturday Review May-June 1983: 41-42.

32. Selection in Anthology

Brater, Enoch. "Ethnics and Ethnicity in the Plays of Arthur Miller."

    From Hester Street to Hollywood: The Jewish-American Stage and

    Screen. Ed. Sarah Blacker Cohen. Bloomington: Indiana UP, 1983.

    123-36.

33. Series _____

Matzer, John, Jr., ed. <u>Capital Financing Strategies for Local Govern-</u>
     <u>ments</u>. Practical Management Series. Washington, DC: International
     City Management Assn., 1983.

34. Subtitle _____

Sundquist, Eric J. <u>Faulkner: The House Divided</u>. Baltimore: Johns
     Hopkins UP, 1983.

Benedict, Helen. "Bernard Malamud: Morals and Surprises." <u>Antioch</u>
     <u>Review</u>, 41 (1983): 28-36.

35. Television or Radio Program _____

<u>Arthur C. Clarke's Mysterious World</u>. PBS TV, Miami. 20 Oct. 1983.

<u>CBS Evening News</u>. Dan Rather. CBS TV. 9 Nov. 1983.

<u>Larry King Show</u>. WGBS Radio. 4 Oct. 1983.

   The title of a radio or television program, underlined, comes first in an entry. It
is followed by the network and the date. Other information, such as the name of a
writer or a producer, if pertinent to a paper, can follow the title.

36. Title within a Title _____

Ringler, Ellin. "<u>Middlemarch</u>: A Feminist Perspective." <u>Studies in the</u>
     <u>Novel</u> 15 (1983): 55-61.

Ruddick, Lisa. "'Melanctha' and the Psychology of William James."
     <u>Modern Fiction Studies</u> 28 (1982-83): 545-56.

"<u>The American Scholar</u>" <u>Today: Emerson's Essay and Some Critical Views</u>.
     Ed. C. David Mead. New York: Dodd, 1970.

Mandel, Oscar. <u>Annotations to</u> Vanity Fair. Washington, DC: UP of
     America, 1981.

The above examples illustrate a book title within a quoted title, a quoted title within a quoted title, a quoted title within a book title, and a book title within a book title. In the latter instance, the shorter title is not underlined.

37. Translation _____

Beauvoir, Simone de. When Things of the Spirit Come First. Trans.

　　　Patrick O'Brien. New York: Pantheon, 1982.

Lattimore, Richard, trans. The Iliad of Homer. Chicago: U Chicago P,

　　　1962.

38. Untitled Article _____

Time. 19 Sept. 1983: 82.

39. Volume Number _____

Blotner, Joseph. Faulkner: A Biography. 2 vols. New York: Random,

　　　1974. Vol. 2.

Edel, Leon. Henry James. 5 vols.　Philadelphia: Lippincott, 1953-72.

Edel, Leon. The Treacherous Years: 1895-1901. Vol. 4 of Henry James.

　　　5 vols. Philadelphia: Lippincott, 1969.

Keats, John. "Ode to Psyche." Norton Anthology of English Literature.

　　　Ed. M.H. Abrams et al. 4th ed. 2 vols. New York: Norton, 1979. 2:

　　　820-22.

In citing a multivolume work, give the total number of volumes between the title and the publication facts. In citing a portion of a volume in a multivolume work, give the volume and page numbers at the end of the entry.

40. Works by the Same Author _____

Bellow, Saul. The Dean's December. New York: Harper, 1982.

- - - . <u>Humboldt's Gift</u>. New York: Viking, 1975.

- - - . <u>Mr. Sammler's Planet</u>. New York: Viking, 1970.

When you list more than one work by the same author or editor, substitute three spaced hyphens for the name in the second and subsequent entries. Follow the hyphens with a period and two spaces and then write the title. Arrange the works alphabetically.

Miscellaneous Special Sources

If you merely mention a painting or a sonata in your paper, no citation or entry in "Works Cited" is required; but if you discuss it in any detail, documentation is necessary. Some of the out-of-the ordinary sources are illustrated below. The exact form of an entry may depend on the emphasis of your paper.

Cartoon

MacNally. "Prescription for a Saner World." Cartoon. <u>Chicago Tribune</u>

 11 May 1984, final ed. Sec 1: 22.

Price, George. Cartoon. <u>New Yorker</u> 7 May 1984: 55.

Cite a cartoon with the artist's name, which may be incomplete on the drawing; the title in quotation marks; and the identification "Cartoon," neither underlined nor quoted. The rest of the entry follows standard form for a newspaper or magazine.

Computer Software

<u>Investment Tax Analyst</u>. Computer software. New York: Wiley, 1984. IBM,

 128k, VisiCalc 1.1.

Kusmiak, Gene. <u>Bank Street Writer</u>. Computer software and manual. San

 Rafael, CA: Brodenbund, 1983. IBM, 64k, 1.1 or 2.0.

The forms for citing the great variety of commercial computer programs have not been completely standardized. In general, an entry should show the writer of the program, if known; the title, underlined; the identification "Computer software," neither underlined nor quoted; and the distributor or manufacturer. At the end of the entry, add relevant information such as the type of computer for which the program is designed, the number of kilobytes, and the operating system. These items are separated by commas.

Map

West Indies and Central America. Map. Washington, DC: National Geographic Soc., 1981.

> A map, chart, or similar work is cited like an anonymous book.

Musical Score

Bach, Johann Sebastian. Brandenburg Concerti. New York: Broude, n.d.

Mozart, Wolfgang Amadeus. Concerto in D Major for Flute and Piano. San Antonio, TX: Southern Music Co., n.d.

> The title of a musical work is underlined, but an instrumental composition identified only by form, number, and key is not underlined or quoted. A published score is listed like a book.

Performance

The Real Thing. By Tom Stoppard. Dir. Mike Nichols. With Jeremy Irons and Glen Close. Plymouth Theatre, New York. 3 May 1984.

Tamasburo. Kabuki Dancers. Japan House, New York. 10 May 1984.

Bernstein, Leonard, cond. New York Philharmonic Orchestra. Copland-Schumann-Stravinsky program. Avery Fisher Hall, New York. 23 May 1984.

> The listing for a performance usually begins with the title, underlined; lists key names involved in production and performance; and closes with the theatre and the city and the date of the performance. The theatre and city are separated by a comma; all other elements are separated by periods. If a paper focuses on an individual, that name can be placed before the title.

Work of Art

Peale, Charles Willson. Staircase Group. Philadelphia Museum of Art, Philadelphia.

Turner, J.M.W. Snowstorm. Tate Gallery, London. Illus. 11 in Landscape Painting of the 19th Century. By Marco Valsecchi. Trans. Arthur

A. Coppotelli. Greenwich CT: New York Graphic Society, 1969.

Homer, Winslow. Snap the Whip. Butler Art Institute, Youngstown, Ohio.

Slide PB 590. New York: Sandak, n.d.

In listing a painting or a work of sculpture, give the artist's name first. Underline the title and identify the museum and the city. If you use a reproduction of the work, add your source and publication data. The best means of coping with a complicated source like the second one above is to look for a simpler one containing the same painting.

CITING SOURCES

Your obligation is the same in any system of documentation: you must cite the specific sources of all borrowed facts and opinions, whether they are quoted or paraphrased. The list of sources in "Works Cited" is a general acknowledgment of indebtedness; specific citations indicate precisely where you found each borrowed item.

Except for some details like omission of the abbreviations "vol." and "p." the new MLA forms in "Works Cited" are not drastically different from conventional bibliographical forms. The method of citing borrowed material, however, is a more radical change and is far more efficient than the use of footnotes or endnotes. Essentially the method is Internal Citation, described earlier (E, pp. 136–37). A typical citation consists of the author's last name and the page reference:(Bernard 346). The parenthetical citation follows quotation marks and precedes any punctuation of your own. By glancing at the "Works Cited" listing, a reader can identify a source with no difficulty.

Explanation notes, if any are needed, are keyed to the text by superscripts and written on a separate page immediately after the final page of the paper. The heading is simply "Notes" and is not quoted or underlined. A simple reference note can be written internally:(see Cecil 134). The book by David Cecil would be listed in "Works Cited." If a reference note includes several sources or a comment long enough to clog the flow of your sentences, it should be written as an endnote. Many student papers require no endnotes.

The identification of a source should be as simple as possible. It consists of the first element in the entry in "Works Cited" (usually the author's last name) and the page reference.

The samples below illustrate the most common forms of citation. These forms and variations on them are also illustrated in the second version of the sample paper (pp. 214–26).

In the type of citation most frequently needed in a paper, the last name of the author of a book or an article and a page reference are enclosed in parentheses and written immediately after the borrowed passage.

Research indicates that ethnic awareness "tends to become an almost

recreational--even quaint--reminder of temps perdu rather than, as in

the older generation, a passionate reality" (Bernard 346).

Coleridge's "Xanadu resembles Milton's prelapsarian Eden both in the

tangible details . . . and in its moral ambiguity" (Tapscott 27).

If the author is clearly identified in the text of your paper, it need not be repeated in the citation.

Jessie Bernard describes the demeaning portrayal of women in soap

operas and situation comedies and points out that most of them are

written and produced by men (454-56).

A general reference to an entire work does not require a parenthetical citation. The work would, of course, be listed in "Works Cited."

Jessie Bernard has described the status of women from a sociological

point of view, and she concludes that women must struggle to overcome

preconceptions and prejudices created by a male-dominated culture.

An anonymous work is cited by a short form of its title.

(Critical Fable 23)

("Coping" 11)

For a work by two or three authors or editors, the last names of all are cited. For a work by three or more persons, the first is cited, followed by *et al.*

(Chancellor and Mears 96)

(Shafritz et al. 107)

A multivolume work is cited as follows:

Faulkner compared Hemingway to "a poker player who kept his cards

close to the vest; he never made mistakes in fact, style, or diction"

(Blotner 2:1231).

If more than one work by the same author is cited, a short form of the title is included.

Faulkner wrote to Hemingway on 28 June 1947 explaining that he was not speaking for publication when he ranked him below Wolfe and DosPassos and was "just making $250.00" (Blotner, <u>Letters</u> 251-52).

A double reference (see **J,** p. 138) is accomplished very simply.

Faulkner's fierce desire for privacy is suggested by what he described as his "lifetime ambition to be the last private individual on earth" (letter to Hamilton Basso qtd. in Blotner 2:1261).

The new style simplifies the citation of quotations from a literary work. Note in the example below that divisions of a work like act, scene, and lines are separated by unspaced periods.

Hamlet describes a realistic acting style when he tells the players to "Speak the speech . . . trippingly on the tongue" (3.2.1-2) and to "Suit the action to the word, the word to the action" (3.2.17-18).

After a little practice, you will overcome such habits as writing "p." before a page number, and you will find that the new style saves time and effort both for you and for your readers.

ABBREVIATIONS AND REFERENCE WORDS

In the documentation and occasionally in the text of a research paper, various abbreviations and reference words are acceptable. Consistency and clearness are essential in the use of these forms. None should be used that do not save space and the reader's time.

For some years there has been a trend away from Latin forms. *Vide* is an example of an unnecessary Latin reference word, for it contains one more letter than its English equivalent (See) and in addition must be underlined. You will find some Latin forms useful in writing your paper, and you will need to know others because they will occur in your reading.

variant   Latin words and abbreviations listed below are underlined to indicate italics. Although there is an increasing trend away from this practice, it is still generally observed in student writing. You should learn and follow the preference of your instructor. In a manuscript that is to be printed, foreign words and abbreviations are often not underlined so that decisions concerning italics can be made by an editor. The following abbreviations might be used in the text of a paper:

A.D.   *anno Domini,* in the year of the Lord (precedes numerals: *A.D.* 1984)

B.C.   before Christ (follows numerals: 547 *B.C.*)

e.g.   *exempli gratia,* for example (preceded and followed by a comma; sometimes confused with *i.e.*)

etc.   *et cetera,* and so forth (avoid using; do not write as *&c.* or as and *etc.*)

i.e.   *id est,* that is (preceded and followed by a comma)

viz.   *videlicet,* namely (sometimes written without a period)

v. vs.   *versus,* against (often not underlined)

The following forms are often used in the documentation of research papers:

anon.   anonymous

c. ca.   *circa,* about (used with approximate dates: *c.* 1340)

cf.   *confer,* compare (used chiefly in a reference note to call attention to a contradictory opinion in another source)

cp.   compare

ch. chs.   chapter, chapters

col. cols.	column, columns
comp.	compiler, compiled by
ed. eds.	editor, edition, edited by; editors, editions
f. ff.	and the following page, pages (used after a page number, but pp. 31–38 is more meaningful than p. 31ff.)
fig. figs.	figure, figures
illus.	illustrated by, illustrator, illustration
introd.	introduction, introduction by
l. ll.	line, lines
MS. MSS.	manuscript, manuscripts (sometimes written without a period)
n. nn.	note, notes (p. 26n. means a note on page 26)
n.d.	no date of publication
no.	number
n.p.	no place of publication when used before the colon in a citation; no publisher when used after the colon
n.pag.	no pagination
p. pp.	page, pages (omitted in some styles of documentation if page numbers alone are clear)
pref.	preface
qtd.	quoted
sic	thus, so (written in brackets within a quotation after an obvious error [*sic*])
trans.	translation, translated by, translator
vol. vols.	volume, volumes (capitalized when used with a number: Vol. 3)

The following forms are seldom used in student writing, but you should be familiar with them because you will encounter them frequently in your reading:

abr.	abridged
aet.	*aetatis,* at the age of
ALS	autograph letter signed
ante	before
app.	appendix
approx.	approximate, approximately
art. arts.	article, articles
b.	born

bibliog.	bibliography, bibliographer
biog.	biography
bk.	book
bull.	bulletin
ⓒ	copyright (followed by a year)
d.	died
dept.	department
diss.	dissertation
doc. docs.	document, documents
enl.	enlarged
esp.	especially (as in see pp. 62–81, esp. p. 79.)
et al.	*et alii,* and others (used for more than three authors: Grove, John, *et al.*)
et seq.	*et sequens,* and the following
fl.	*floruit,* flourished, lived (used when dates of birth and death are unknown: *fl.* 1182–1201)
front.	frontispiece
Ibid.	*ibidem,* in the same place (used only in notes, always the first word in a note and therefore always capitalized); its use has declined in recent years.
idem	the same as previously mentioned
infra	below
jour.	journal
loc. cit.	*loco citato,* in the place cited (properly used in the text to refer to a passage recently cited; never followed by a page number)
mag.	magazine
N.B.	*nota bene,* mark well, take careful note (usually not advisable in student papers)
narr.	narration, narrated by, narrator
n.s.	new series (used with periodicals)
N.S.	New Style (used when necessary for a date after 1752 reckoned by the Gregorian calendar)
obs.	obsolete
op. cit.	*opere citato,* in the work cited (used only in footnotes and only after an author's name); seldom used at present.

o.s.	old series, original series (used with periodicals)
O.S.	Old Style (used when necessary for a date before 1752 reckoned by the Julian calendar)
passim	here and there throughout a work (used for scattered references: Ch. Six *passim* or pp. 145–56 *et passim*)
per se	in or by itself (Avoid using if possible.)
post	after
pseud.	pseudonym
pt. pts.	part, parts
q.v.	*quod vide,* which see (used in the text or in a note for a cross-reference)
rev.	review, reviewed by; revision, revised by (Write out if ambiguous.)
rpt.	reprint, reprinted
sc. scs.	scene, scenes
scil.	*scilicet,* namely
ser.	series
st. sts.	stanza, stanzas
sup.	*supra,* above
supp.	supplement
s.v.	*sub verbo,* under the word (used to refer to an item in an alphabetical listing)
TLS	typewritten letter signed
v. vid.	*vide,* see

In a note or a bibliography entry, a state more than four letters long is abbreviated after the name of a city; elsewhere a state should be written out. Conventional forms are listed on the left, but the two-letter postal forms (written without periods) are gaining acceptance.

Ala.	AL	Me.	ME	Okla.	OK
Ariz.	AZ	Md.	MD	Oreg.	OR
Ark.	AR	Mass.	MA	Pa.	PA
Calif.	CA	Mich.	MI	R.I.	RI
Colo.	CO	Minn.	MN	S.C.	SC
Conn.	CT	Miss.	MS	S.Dak.	SD
Del.	DE	Mo.	MO	Tenn.	TN
D.C.	DC	Mont.	MT	Tex.	TX
Fla.	FL	Nebr.	NE	Utah	UT
Ga.	GA	Nev.	NV	Vt.	VT
Ida.	ID	N.H.	NH	Va.	VA
Ill.	IL	N.J.	NJ	Wash.	WA
Ind.	IN	N.Mex.	NM	W.Va.	WV
Iowa	IA	N.Y.	NY	Wisc.	WI
Kans.	KS	N.C.	NC	Wyo.	WY
Ky.	KY	N.Dak.	ND		
La.	LA	Ohio	OH		

Exercise O   Preparing a Bibliography

Unscramble the bibliographical data below and arrange the eight entries in good bibliographical form.

1. A news item on page 17 of the New York Times for the 3rd of March, 1944.

2. An article entitled Casablanca in the journal Films and Filming for August 1974 on pages 20 to 29 of volume 20. It was written by Barry Day.

3. A biography entitled Humphrey Bogart written by Nathaniel Benchley and published in 1973 by Little, Brown Co. of Boston.

4. An article in Time by Lance Morrow entitled We'll Always Have Casablanca on page 76 of the December 27, 1982, issue.

5. An essay by Richard Schickel entitled Some Nights in Casablanca published in a book edited by Philip Nobile entitled Favorite Movies with the subtitle Critics' Choice; it was published by Macmillan Co. of New York in 1973, and the essay appears on pages 114 to 125.

6. A book by Howard Koch entitled Casablanca, subtitled Script and Legend, published in 1973 by Overlook Press of Woodstock, New York.

7. An article by Ronald Haver entitled Finally the Truth about Casablanca, published on pages 10 to 16 of the first volume of American Film in the June 1976 issue.

8. A book by Richard Corliss entitled Talking Pictures, subtitled Screenwriters in the American Cinema 1927–1973, published in 1974 by Overlook Press in Woodstock, New York.

Exercise P   Writing Citation Notes

Using the bibliographical data in Exercise O, convert the items below into a sequence of notes in conventional form.

1. Page 112 of the book by Benchley

2. Page 21 of the book by Day

3. Page 51 of the book by Koch

4. Page 56 of the book by Koch

5. Page 106 of the article by Corliss

6. Page 16 of the article by Haver

7. Page 19 of the article by Day

8. Page 87 of the book by Koch

SIX
WRITING THE PAPER

A man may write at any time, if he will set himself doggedly to it.

After you have spent many hours compiling a bibliography, taking notes, and constructing an outline, the actual writing of the paper may seem an anticlimax, but it is the most important phase of the writing process because your work will be judged on the basis of your writing skill. Writing is an individualistic activity that cannot be condensed into a series of formal steps. No two persons write in the same way, and each writing assignment presents special problems. Suggestions in this chapter are not offered as mechanical steps in a formula. Try them and adopt those that work well for you.

THE ROUGH DRAFT

It is impossible to judge your material while it exists only in your mind and on note cards. When you have set it down in a rough draft, you will have something tangible that you can evaluate and revise. Do not attempt to write the final version of your paper from the note cards. Only a few professional writers are fortunate enough to be capable of writing acceptable prose without making at least one preliminary draft.

Getting Started

Collecting material for your paper will take time, but it should not be prolonged unduly. If you feel reluctant to begin the actual writing, filling stacks of note cards in the library may be a way of postponing the task: procrastination disguised by a false sense of accomplishment. At any rate, there is a point of diminishing returns in research, and when you have investigated your topic thoroughly you should start the rough draft. There are no ideal conditions for writing, but your job will be easier if you can find a place where you can work without interruption or distraction. Try to allot several hours to the rough draft so that you can get it on paper in a single sitting.

Organizing and Writing

When you begin composing the first draft, the value of taking notes on cards should become apparent. On a tabletop or on the floor if necessary, spread out the cards and sort them into piles that correspond to the main headings of your outline. If you have labeled the note cards, this sorting process will be simplified. In classifying your note cards, you must be reconciled to two grim facts:

1. **Some note cards will be eliminated.** Anyone writing a research paper takes some notes on speculation. You may use only two-thirds of the notes you have taken. Throw away those that are clearly useless. Put doubtful ones in a special pile for later consideration. In any construction some waste is inevitable; a research paper is no exception. Squeezing every note into a paper merely because of the time and energy spent in recording it will destroy the unity of your paper.
2. **Some additional reading will be necessary.** As you work out the detailed structure of your paper, you are likely to find weak spots that need to be reinforced. You may have to return to some of your sources to obtain additional material or to check references. You may also have to locate new sources to supplement your notes.

When you are ready to begin writing, check your main points to be certain that they all clearly pertain to your thesis and that they follow a logical order. Then look through the cards supporting your first main point to determine the most logical and effective arrangement. If you have not already done so in a preliminary outline, vary the development of the paragraphs. If one is arranged chronologically, try to follow a different arrangement in the next.

When the piles of note cards are arranged in the order of use, you are ready to begin the actual writing. If possible, finish the draft in a single session and resist the temptation to postpone writing until another day. Do not lose your momentum by lingering over the choice of words; if you come to an idea that you find difficult to express, leave enough space for it and go on. As you write, keep looking ahead in your notes, trying to anticipate transitions that will connect your ideas effectively.

Although they are products of an affluent society, many students are incredibly stingy with paper, cramming as many words as possible on each page and even writing on both sides. Such a crowded page is almost impossible to revise. Be generous with space; leave wide margins on both sides or triple-space so that you can add or change material.

Be meticulous about copying quotations exactly as they appear on your note cards, about checking the wording of all quotations against the original source, and about the placement of quotation marks and ellipses. If you have a fairly long quotation, clip the note card to the page at the spot where it will be used. Copying and recopying it would just multiply the chances of errors creeping in.

In a rough draft it is not advisable to write out footnotes or endnotes in their full form. If you revise the draft drastically, you may overlook some notes when you recopy it. The simplest procedure is to write a brief citation in parentheses (Miller 67) immediately after the borrowed passage. This procedure is necessary and natural, of course, if you are using the new MLA style of documentation. Before making another draft, be certain that you have citations for all borrowed material. If you encircle the citations with a red pencil, you will be less likely to overlook any of them when you write the next draft. In preparing the final copy, use your bibliography cards to expand each citation, working page by page if you are using footnotes and listing notes on a separate sheet after completing the draft if you are using endnotes.

Revise your rough draft frequently and do not worry much about neatness. Even if it is handed in with the paper, a rough draft is not expected to be a thing of beauty. Whether or not a second draft is needed will depend on your own writing habits and the legibility of your handwriting. If you revise extensively, you may need to make an intermediate version.

Managing Quotations

A poor research paper is often a scissors-and-paste collection of quotations looming up at intervals in student prose. One of the marks of a superior paper is that quotations are smoothly blended into the text instead of standing alone with no clear connection to what precedes or to what follows. The graceful incorporation of borrowed material into the text is a major concern in revision, but a beginning can be made in the rough draft. One reason for awkwardness with quotations may be uncertainty about mechanics. Be certain that you understand the following conventions:

1. A quotation in the text of a paper is enclosed in double quotation marks. A quotation within a quotation is enclosed in single quotation marks. If you quote a passage that contains double quotation marks, change them to singles and use doubles to enclose the passage. Some publishers, especially in England, enclose quotations in single quotation marks—the reverse of American practice. It is permissible, for the sake of consistency, to change them to doubles.
2. The colon is a common but rather formal way of introducing a quotation. A verb like "said" or "wrote" introducing a quotation is ordinarily followed by a comma. Some students erroneously extend this rule and place a comma before every quotation. When the word "that" precedes a quotation, a comma is seldom necessary. Three common ways of introducing short quotations are illustrated below:

Andrew Carnegie frankly stated his justification for the inequality of

wealth: "The condition of the masses is satisfactory just in proportion as a country is blessed with millionaires."[1]

Andrew Carnegie wrote, "The condition of the masses is satisfactory just in proportion as a country is blessed with millionaires."[1]

Andrew Carnegie sincerely believed "the condition of the masses is satisfactory just in proportion as a country is blessed with millionaires."[1]

3. A quotation of four lines or more is usually written in block or display form. It is indented ten spaces, single-spaced, and not enclosed in quotation marks unless *variant* they appear in the original. Your instructor may prefer that you double-space block quotations, the proper form in a manuscript that is to be printed. The block form calls attention to a quotation and thereby emphasizes it somewhat. Block quotations are illustrated in the sample paper (pp. 199–203). The following example of a block quotation is taken from two paragraphs in "Montaigne; or, The Skeptic," an essay by Emerson:

> Society does not like to have any breath of question blown on the existing order. But the interrogation of custom at all points is an inevitable stage in the growth of every superior mind. . . .
>   The superior mind will find itself equally at odds with the evils of society and with the projects that are offered to relieve them. The wise skeptic is a bad citizen; no conservative, he sees the selfishness of property and the drowsiness of institutions. But neither is he fit to work with any democratic party that ever was constituted; for parties wish every one committed, and he penetrates the popular patriotism. . . . It stands in his mind that our life in this world is not of quite so easy interpretation as churches and schoolbooks say.[1]

The first ellipsis marks the omission of eighteen words. The fourth line is indented because it is the beginning of a new paragraph in the original. Three sentences are omitted after the word "patriotism."

4. A quotation must be an exact reproduction of the original, but if the meaning or the emphasis of the original is not distorted, the following exceptions are possible:

a. An initial capital letter may be reduced to lowercase if only a portion of a sentence is quoted.
b. A word or a brief phrase enclosed in brackets may be inserted for clarity.
c. A final punctuation mark may be dropped.
d. Words may be omitted if the omission is signalled by an ellipsis, three spaced periods (. . .).

The purpose of all four exceptions is to facilitate the blending of quoted material with your own sentence, as in the following example:

```
Skepticism, according to Emerson, involves "the interrogation of
custom at all points."2
```

An ellipsis is not necessary at the beginning or end of a brief passage if the meaning of the original is not altered. The identification of a source in a phrase like "according to Emerson" should be submerged within a quotation if possible.

5. Brackets rather than parentheses are used to enclose material interpolated by the writer of a paper.

```
"It stands in his [the skeptic's] mind that our life in this world is
not of quite so easy interpretation as churches and schoolbooks say."3
```

THE FINAL COPY

Revision is a highly important but often neglected step in the writing process. Too many students, when asked to revise a paper, assume that they are simply expected to recopy it neatly, add a few commas, and correct any spelling errors. Actually, effective revision is just as creative as the initial act of writing.

Effective Revision

To revise a paper effectively, you must see it from a reader's point of view. If time permits, put the rough draft aside for a few days before revising it. Immediately after you finish writing, your mind is so filled with what you wanted to say that you are a poor judge of what you actually said. A cooling-off period will enable you to judge your essay more objectively. In reading over your draft, try to assume the role of an uninformed, semireluctant reader whose interest must be aroused and whose attention must be held.

Unlike the rough draft, which should be written in one sitting if possible, the final version should be revised a page or two at a time. The advantage of piecemeal revision is that you can concentrate on details. Carry the draft in your notebook and write in changes or additions as they occur to you. An elusive word or an effective combination of unwieldy sentence elements may pop into your mind at unexpected times. One of the ironies of composition is that such flashes of inspiration quickly fade from the memory. Try to write them down as they occur to you.

If you want to add a lengthy passage, do not recopy the entire page but write the additional material on a separate sheet, assign it a code letter, and indicate where it should be inserted: Insert C. This technique and others are illustrated below by a portion of the rough draft of the sample paper. The changes involve correction of punctuation and spelling, addition of details, rearrangement of sentence elements, and substitution of more accurate language for general phrasing. Compare it with the fifth paragraph of the final version (pp. 195–97).

Custer's defeat ~~carried emotional appeal.~~

Other aspects of the battle stirred people's

sympathy. ③ ~~Two~~ of his brothers, a brother-in-law,

a ② {K ①
and his nephew were killed with Custer.) The grief

of Mrs. Custer stirred the nation's sympathy. The

~~alleged~~ on *squaws*
supposed mutilating of the bodies by the Sioux ^ added

e *In*
a ^ grusome touch. Writing a letter to the Helena

enant ,
Daily Herald, Lieut. James H. Bradley ^ who discovered

denied
the bodies, said that ~~not~~ many of them were mutilated

(Graham, Story, p. 166), but Indian experts all over the

refuted him.
country ~~denied it.~~ In the legend the bodies had to

's men   (Stories of the
be mutilated. ^ General Terry buried the officers in   subsequent fate
                                                          of the bodies
                                                          persisted for years)
shallow graves but left many enlisted men unburied.

← Insert E

Markers were later set up by guesswork (Montana, p. 263).

legend ← Insert F
The claims of survivors also kept the ~~story~~ alive.

According to Lawrence A. Frost, over 200 men turned up

various *ing*
at different times and claimed to have survived the battle.

Check each paragraph to make certain that it is unified around a single idea and that it is developed in logical sequence. Be certain that the steps in the development are logical and correspond to your outline.

Transitions between paragraphs and between subtopics within a paragraph should be clear. You probably need more transitional material than you think you do. As the writer of a paper, you are like a driver on a familiar highway who does not need to watch for signs and landmarks, but the reader will be like someone driving on a strange road who needs directional markers. You are so familiar with your material that you know what is coming next, and it is easy to underestimate the amount of guidance a reader will need. It is better to be over-obvious than to be obscure. Comments facing the sample paper (pp. 188–203) discuss various transitional devices.

The most effective transitions are often organic ones that derive from the material itself. Transitional elements are words and phrases that indicate relationships among ideas. The following table lists some kinds of relationships and some transitional elements that express them:

continuation or *addition* accordingly, again, along with, also, and, as well as, besides, first, second (not firstly, secondly, now reserved chiefly for sermons), furthermore, in addition, last, likewise, moreover, next, too

opposition or *contrast* but, however, in contrast, on the contrary, on the other hand, otherwise, yet

agreement or *comparison* in like manner, in the same way, just as, like, similarly

time after, afterward, always, during, in the meantime, later, meanwhile, never, next, now, sometimes, then, when, while

place above, adjacent to, below, beyond, here, nearby, there, where, wherever

cause or *reason* as a consequence, because, consequently, due to, owing to, since

effect or *result* accordingly, as a result, consequently, hence, then, therefore, thus

purpose in order to, so that

qualification almost, however, perhaps, probably

condition although, at any rate, even though, if, in case, nevertheless, nonetheless, on condition that, provided that

summary in conclusion, in short, to sum up

The ideas in the left-hand column obviously do not represent all the relationships that may exist among ideas. Although the transitional elements grouped together are similar in meaning, no two are identical. Sensitivity to nuances of meaning and the ability to choose the appropriate transitional device can be developed by attentive reading and by practice in writing.

Your instructor will undoubtedly specify the level of formality appropriate to your paper. In a highly formal style, contractions and the pronouns "I" and "you" are not used, but referring to yourself as "the writer" or "this researcher" is usually clumsy. Formality may also encourage overuse of the passive voice. The stylistic level should be appropriate to your topic and your thesis.

Sentences should be revised for clarity and correctness and especially for variety. There is a tendency in research papers to write sentences that are monotonously alike. Try to vary your sentences in structure, arrangement, and length. Sentence beginnings are especially important since there is a natural inclination to start every sentence with the subject. Moving a subordinate clause or a prepositional phrase to the beginning often improves clarity as well as the sound of a sentence. Avoid, however, starting too many sentences with transitional elements. They should be submerged within the sentence if possible, especially between the subject and the verb or the verb and its object.

A topic for a research paper will almost always involve terms and expressions that are not part of your everyday active vocabulary. Be certain that you use them accurately. At any given time, a few terms ("buzz words") seem to be fashionable in the academic world, and because they are used so often, they are often used loosely. If you use a word like "charisma," "continuum," "counterproductive," "input," "rationale," "supportive," "syndrome," or "viable," be sure that it expresses the meaning you intend. Avoid using "hopefully" as a sentence-modifier; "thrust" as a noun; "contact," "impact," "implement," and "program" as verbs; and the innumerable combinations that result from attaching words to the prefix "mini-" or to the suffix "-wise."

Wordiness is a common fault in research papers, probably because students feel pressure to attain a certain number of words. In revision substitute specific words for general ones. Concentrate on the nouns and verbs; if they are exact, fewer modifiers will be needed. Try to eliminate all unnecessary words, especially bloated constructions like the following:

at no time = never
at the conclusion of = after
at the time that = when
at this point in time = now
due to the fact that = because
during the time that = while
for the reason that = because
in a short time = soon
in all likelihood = probably
in spite of = despite
in spite of the fact that = although
in the event that = if
in the place that = where
on or about = approximately
prior to the time that = before

A minor problem that often arises is the form used for names. In general, do not use a title like Mr., Ms, Dr., or Professor with a proper name, but there are a few exceptions for which usage has made the title seem natural: Sir Walter Raleigh, Dr. Johnson, Madame Curie. Cite a person's full name on the first use; afterward use the surname alone. A combination like "Scott and Jane Austen" or "Whitman and Emily Dickinson" may suggest a sexist bias.

At least once during the revision process, read your paper aloud. In reading something as familiar as your draft will be by this time, your eyes have a tendency to glide over it uncritically. Reading aloud slows your eye movement and enables you to notice clumsy constructions and other weaknesses that you might overlook in silent reading. If you find a sentence difficult to read smoothly, it probably should be recast.

A research paper should be typed if possible. If a handwritten copy is acceptable, leave generous margins and write as neatly as you can. If possible, type the final copy yourself. Besides the expense of hiring a typist, there are two disadvantages to having a paper typed by someone else. First, you lose the benefits of last-minute inspiration if someone else types the final copy. The psychological pressure of preparing the final version is sometimes beneficial; problems of expression seem to solve themselves, and disjointed sentence elements fall into their proper places. Second, you place yourself in a kind of double jeopardy: You are responsible for your own errors as well as for those made by the typist. If you do not type the final copy, read and correct your paper carefully before giving it to the typist and again after it has been typed.

Using a Word Processor

If you have access to a word processor and can operate it efficiently, it will facilitate the preparation of your research paper. The chief hazard is losing a portion of your text because you inadvertently press the wrong key or because of a power failure, a faulty disk, or some other calamity. Keep your notes and other back-up materials until the paper has been printed. Be sure to type the "Save" command when you finish typing, and print the paper as soon as possible. In typing your first research paper, you will need a few minutes to habituate yourself to the commands for underlining and for reference numbers. If you type the proper command before and after a title, it will be underlined when printed; but if you forget to type the command after a title, the machine will continue underlining your text until you are able to stop it. Similarly, if you type the "Superscript" command before and after a reference number, it will be elevated a half-space and printed after the cited material.

An advantage of a word processor is that it eliminates the drudgery of recopying a draft. Seeing your text neatly displayed on a screen is much more satisfying than struggling to decipher scribbled words on dog-eared sheets of paper. The major advantage, however, is that a word processor facilitates revision. You can delete, add, or move words simply by pressing the proper keys. Manipulating your text as it appears on the screen is easier and more enjoyable than crossing out words, writing above the lines, and otherwise marking up a rough draft. In this respect, if used efficiently, a word processor can make you a better writer. Remember, however, that vague generalities, inexact words, and awkward constructions are not improved by being produced mechanically. The ideas and language you put into the machine are what really matter. The most important word processing, after all, takes place in your own mind.

Proper Manuscript Form

A research paper is, of course, evaluated primarily on its content, but its appearance is also important. Your instructor will undoubtedly specify some aspects of the format, and you should follow those specifications closely.

Use a good quality of bond paper, 8½ × 11. Material typed on onionskin paper is difficult to read, and typing on "erasable" paper tends to smudge.

A paper is usually fastened in a binder or manila folder. Paper clips are preferable to staples. Write your name, your class section, and the date on the outside of the folder.

Your paper should have a title page. The title should be brief but accurate. It should not be enclosed in quotation marks or underlined. Since college papers usually receive no special credit for decoration, it is futile to waste your time on ribbons, pictures, or fancy lettering. A title page should be neat but not gaudy.

If an outline is required, it should follow the title page. In addition to reviewing its logic, parallelism, and general neatness, check the alignment of Roman numerals. The last rather than the first units should be on the same margin so that the periods align.

Be certain that the pages are in the proper order and that each page is numbered. Use no periods, hyphens, parentheses, or other punctuation with page numbers. On each page with a title or any kind of heading, the page number should be centered at the bottom or omitted. On other pages the number belongs in the upper right-hand corner.

Place a page number one inch from the top of the page. Place a title two inches from the top; double-space twice below the title. Leave margins of an inch at both sides and at the top and bottom of the page.

Indent each paragraph five spaces. If a sentence closes in the last line of a page, continue with the next sentence unless it is the end of a paragraph.

The body of the paper should be double-spaced. Triple-spacing between paragraphs improves the appearance of the paper. Unless your instructor specifies double-spacing of notes, single-space each one and double-space between notes. Both footnotes and endnotes are indented conventionally. Even if they are very short, you should not write two notes on the same line.

Before typing the bibliography, be certain that the cards are in alphabetical order. It would also be prudent to compare your notes with your bibliography cards to make certain that every source cited is included in the bibliography. Hanging indentation is customary in a bibliography entry. The first line is flush with the margin, and each additional line is indented five spaces. As with notes, single-space each entry and double-space between entries.

Proofreading

Proofreading is to revision as paring potatoes is to gourmet cooking—a humdrum and mechanical but essential chore. As in revision, it is advisable to do a page or two at a time and to read the manuscript aloud.

In proofreading a paper, look for typographical errors, misspellings, errors in punctuation and capitalization, and similar slips. Consult your handbook when necessary. An error that occurs surprisingly often is the omission of a word. Although it is a purely mechanical oversight made in copying the paper, it can distort or destroy the meaning of a sentence. Another minor error often overlooked may occur when a word is broken at the end of a line. Words should be separated only between syllables. If you are in doubt concerning the syllabification of a word, consult your dictionary. In fact, do not divide a word unless it is absolutely necessary. A somewhat irregular right margin is preferable to the annoyance of numerous hyphenated words.

Correct errors as neatly as possible, writing corrections above the line and indicating the insertion of material with a caret (^). If a page contains several corrections so that it looks messy, you should recopy it. If you type the paper yourself, scan each page before removing it from the typewriter. Using correction tape or white liquid eraser, you can easily correct simple errors like transposed letters without having to realign the page.

Labour and care are rewarded with success.

SAMPLE RESEARCH PAPER
Conventional Style

The sample research paper that follows has been revised somewhat to illustrate as many aspects of research writing as possible. Because the paper compares different versions of the Custer legend, it contains an unusually large amount of documentation. The number of notes makes it possible to illustrate a variety of forms but may be misleading; a paper on a different topic might have only half as many notes.

Reading the comments would be a useful way of reviewing documentation and other techniques already discussed.

A title page should be simple in appearance with the basic items symmetrically arranged. The title should not be enclosed in quotation marks or underlined.

The writer's last name can also be included on each page just before the page number, but this is seldom necessary in a short paper.

The Custer Legend

by

George Spelvin

English 101 H

April 27, 1984

Outline

On a page bearing a title or any sort of heading, the page number is placed at the bottom or omitted.

In the topic outline on the facing page, each heading is a noun or a noun phrase.

Note that Roman numerals are aligned on the right rather than on the left.

Main heads and subheads (Roman numerals and capital letters) are double-spaced; subordinate headings are single-spaced.

The thesis states the general purpose of the essay—analysis of a legend. Nothing should be admitted to the paper that does not directly or indirectly support this central purpose. A paragraph about Crazy Horse or Sitting Bull, for example, would be out of place unless it could somehow be related to the Custer legend.

Since the thesis suggests a twofold approach to the topic (the battle itself and related aspects), the paper is planned in two sections. The outline, therefore, has three ranks of headings: sections, paragraphs, and subdivisions of paragraphs. Such close correspondence between an outline and a paper is not always necessary or possible. A capital letter, for example, might represent two paragraphs. But when writing your first research paper, you will find it easier and safer to make all symbols of the same rank stand for approximately the same units of the essay.

The working outline for this paper was probably more detailed and may have contained a mixture of sentences and phrases. The final outline shows only the main structure, not the details. A working outline is for the writer's use; a final outline is for the reader's.

The plan of the first section is chronological; strategic planning precedes the battle.

The plan of the second section is analytical, and it was probably much more troublesome to organize. Five aspects of the event that helped make it a legend are arranged in roughly chronological order, proceeding from the news reports just after the battle to movies, paintings, and poems produced later. The arrangement is also climactic, for the last main paragraph contains the most extreme exaggerations in the legend.

Although the essay contains a concluding paragraph, it is not shown in the outline because it is a restatement of the thesis.

The Custer Legend

Thesis: George Armstrong Custer and his defeat at little Big Horn are familiar American legends because of a wide range of imaginative and emotional appeals.

I. The battle

   A. Grand strategy

      1. Western and southern columns
      2. Eastern column

   B. The fight

      1. Division of troops
      2. Reno's fight
      3. Custer's fight

II. The legend

   A. News of the massacre

      1. The West
      2. The East

   B. The personality of Custer

      1. Public figure
      2. National martyr
      3. Tragic hero

   C. Emotional appeals

      1. The Custer family
      2. The bodies
      3. Survivor stories
      4. Comanche

   D. Controversy

      1. Defenders of the army
      2. Custer's defenders
      3. Reno's defense of his actions

   E. Imaginative versions

      1. Movies
      2. Paintings
      3. Poems

1   *It is not absolutely necessary to repeat the title when a paper has a title page.*

2   *The first paragraph expands the thesis. An introductory paragraph should accurately represent the meaning and the emphasis of the thesis statement. An introductory paragraph may not be necessary if the thesis is fairly simple. In that case, the thesis statement is the opening sentence of the first main paragraph.*

3   *one fact from outline note*

Frost   Custer's fame

p. 3   ¼ million visit battlefield
        every summer
p. 7   only Washington and Lincoln
        have been written about more
        than C.

---

4   *The first two sentences state the topic, "Grand strategy." The basis of division is the organization of the military forces involved. The western and southern columns are treated together because they are not of major importance in this paper. General Crook's fight is mentioned because it provides a transition to Custer and the eastern column.*

5   *The summary of the strategy is based on seven pages of a book. Ordinarily such an extended summary should be avoided, but it is necessary in this paragraph and the next to sketch in the event as concisely as possible. A patchwork of facts from several sources would be less clear and would require numerous citation notes.*

6   *"Free of the supervision" recalls "on his own." Repetition of an idea is often a more effective transitional bridge than repetition of a word.*

7   *Since this page has a title, the number is centered at the bottom. Subsequent pages are numbered in the upper right-hand corner.*

(indent 5 spaces)

1   The Custer Legend

quadruple-space

2   All Americans have heard of Custer's Last Stand. Many cherish a romantic
but inaccurate vision of George Armstrong Custer wielding his saber against the

3 onrushing Sioux. The battle has been described many times, and more has been

approx. 1"

written about Custer than any American except Washington and Lincoln.[1] Both the
battle and Custer himself are familiar because they are legends. A legend
develops because of a wide range of imaginative and emotional appeals.

triple-space

4   The Custer legend began as a simple maneuver in a large-scale operation.

5 The plan called for three columns to converge on the Sioux, who had left their
reservations. A column from the west under Colonel John Gibbon was to start
from Fort Ellis, Montana, and a column under General George Crook was to
advance from the south. General Crook encountered Sioux on the Rosebud River
and was forced to withdraw after a fierce fight. Neither Custer nor his
commander, General Alfred H. Terry, knew about this battle. Their column,
commanded by General Terry, left Fort Abraham Lincoln, Dakota Territory, on
May 17, 1876. Where the Rosebud empties into the Yellowstone River, Terry
joined Gibbon's column. Terry ordered Gibbon to march south along the Little
Big Horn. Custer was to follow the Rosebud, swing west, and march north along
the Little Big Horn. The Sioux would thus be caught between two forces. Terry
accompanied Gibbon's troops.[2] Custer was on his own.

6   Free of the supervision of his commander, Custer apparently sought battle
as speedily as possible. He twice divided his forces. On June 25, though

7   2

8   The paragraph plan divides the events of June 25 into three phases: the division of the troops, Reno's fight, and Custer's fight.

9   Maps, diagrams, graphs, or other illustrative material may clarify a passage in a paper. They should not be used merely for decoration. The credit line for an illustration is placed directly beneath it rather than at the bottom of the page. No reference number is used. Whether the graphic material is traced or copied from a source or based on information found in a source, an acknowledgment is necessary. The credit line follows the form of a primary note.

10   If several illustrations are included, they can be placed in an appendix. If more than one is used, they should be labeled Figure 1, Figure 2, etc. When necessary, reference to these labels can be made in the text of the paper.

11   The student faced a minor dilemma in describing both Reno's and Custer's actions since they occurred almost simultaneously. "Custer's fate" points ahead to the next subtopic. The tense of the verbs "had been lost" and "had veered" also clarifies the transition from Reno to Custer.

12   quotation note

Luce, p. 18 + photo p. 22   battle
message carried by John Martin
"Benteen -- Come on -- Big village --
Be quick -- Bring packs -- W. W. Cooke
P.S. Bring pacs."
                                          adjutant
    sic

13   Note the brackets around the identification of W. W. Cooke, which the student supplied. It was, perhaps, unnecessary to call attention to the misspelling of "packs" by following it with **sic.**

8 warned by his scouts that a Sioux village lay ahead, he sent Captain F. W. Benteen to the left with three troops. One troop brought up the rear with the packs. Three troops were assigned to Major M. A. Reno. The remaining five troops were under Custer himself. Benteen's party was soon hidden by high bluffs and cottonwood trees. After about two hours Custer again divided his force, sending Reno across the river. Reno attacked the Sioux village and after hard fighting withdrew to the eastern bank. He took refuge on high ground, where he was later joined by Benteen. They were pinned down and knew

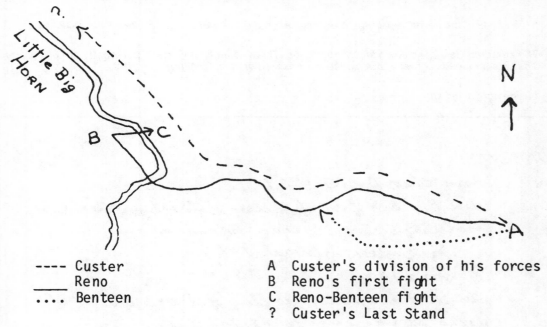

9
10

```
---- Custer          A  Custer's division of his forces
____ Reno            B  Reno's first fight
.... Benteen         C  Reno-Benteen fight
                     ?  Custer's Last Stand
```

Based on Edward S. Luce and Evelyn S. Luce, Custer Battlefield National Monument, Montana (Washington, D.C.: National Park Service, 1952), p. 13.

11 nothing of Custer's fate until Gibbon reached them on June 27. Custer had been lost from sight before Reno's troops charged. He had veered to the right, perhaps to attack the village from another direction. Soon he must have realized that his scouts had been correct. A hastily scribbled note was sent

12 by courier: "Benteen -- Come on -- Big Village -- Be quick -- Bring packs.

13 W. W. Cooke [Custer's adjutant]. P.S. Bring pacs [sic]." The message to

14 Except for the last sentence, all of the paragraph is a summary based on a single source. There is no standard way of indicating the beginning of a borrowed summary except to introduce it with a phrase like "According to Edward and Evelyn Luce . . . ". Such acknowledgments are rather awkward and can be omitted if the context makes clear how much has been summarized. Here the reader would assume that the entire paragraph except the last sentence is based on the Luce book.

15 The sentence serves as a bridge between the two main divisions of the paper.

16 The first sentence is transitional. The second is the topic sentence. The basis of division is spatial (West and East).

17 Usage varies somewhat in respect to numerals. Generally, with the exception of statistics, page numbers, and dates, numbers that can be written in one or two words are written out. Numerals are used for those requiring more than two words (180).

18 The effect of the news is conjecture and does not require a citation. Expressions like "must have been" and "probably" indicate that these statements are opinions, not facts.

19 "The shock of the news" recalls the previous paragraph. The word "also" is likewise transitional.

20 The paragraph is organized on an abstract basis. Three aspects of Custer's personality are discussed. They are arranged in order of climax, the most exalted or most fanciful coming last.

21 outline note summarized

DAB, V   biog
p. 7   born Ohio Dec. 5, 1839
        West Point -- "foot of a class of thirty-four" 1861
        noticed by McClellan, Pleasanton
            brigadier-general 1863
            major   "   1864
        pursued Lee, received flag of truce apr. 9, '65
p. 8   defeated Cheyennes at Washita 1868
        discovered gold in Black Hills 1874
        testified vs War Dept. March 1876
p. 9   sketches in Galaxy. > My Life on the Plains 1875

---

22 The arrangement is chronological. Long biographical digressions are a pitfall in a paper like this. The summary of Custer's career includes only actions that contributed to the legend.

Benteen is the last verifiable word from Custer. His entire command was wiped
14 out. The bodies were discovered on June 27 by Gibbon's men.[3] With Custer's
15 futile appeal to Benteen, fact stops and legend begins.

From the beginning the Custer story seemed destined to become a legend.
16 Even the way the news broke was spectacular. News of the battle did not reach
the outside world until July 4. A scout named Taylor carried the news from the
battlefield. Accounts differ, but in one of the most impressive, a rancher
17 named Horace Countryman rode 180 miles with only one change of horses to reach
Helena, Montana, with Taylor's story. Such a heroic exploit suits a legend.
Andrew J. Fisk, editor of the Helena Daily Herald, rounded up enough celebrating
printers to issue a special edition.[4] Eastern newspapers carried the story on
18 July 6. In Washington and Philadelphia the centennial of independence had just
been celebrated. To a nation still in a holiday mood, the catastrophe must
have been a stunning shock. Many people probably remembered the Custer defeat
all their lives because of the ironic coincidence of its occurring just before
the Centennial Fourth of July.

19   The shock of the news was also intensified by Custer's celebrity. He had
20 been in the public eye for nearly fifteen years. After graduating at the
bottom of his West Point class in 1861, he attracted the attention of several
21 ranking officers and advanced rapidly. As a temporary major general, known
22 for his colorful uniforms and long blond hair, he led the pursuit of Lee's army
in the last days of the Civil War and received the first flag of truce. In
1868 he defeated a band of Cheyennes at the Battle of Washita. His exploration
of the Black Hills in 1874 inspired a gold rush. Frontier sketches that he
wrote for The Galaxy made up a best-selling book, My Life on the Plains,

23 The transitional signpost pointing to the second subdivision is "Yet," and "however" points to the third.

24 The second and third subdivisons are mainly speculative opinion. The tentative nature of some of the ideas is suggested by "may have," "Perhaps," and "probably."

25 "Furthermore" and "Finally" are transitional signals.

26 The first sentence echoes "stirred people's emotions" and is also the topic sentence. The organization is analytical: four emotional aspects of the legend. The arrangement proceeds from the most serious to the least. This order is somewhat risky because of the potentially ludicrous effect of anticlimax.

27 The discussion of the bodies is probably too long. A writer can easily be misled into expanding unduly a topic that has some grotesque, comic or otherwise intriguing aspect.

28 quotation converted to summary

Graham, _Story_, p. 166   bodies

Lieut. James H. Bradley, letter to _Helena Weekly_
Herald, July 27, 1876

"Of the 206 bodies buried on the field, there
were very few that I did not see, and
beyond scalping, in possibly a majority
of cases, there was little mutilation.
Many of the bodies were not even scalped..."

29 Words occasionally may be underlined for emphasis or for clarity. The practice can become a bad habit if overdone, but the underlining of "had" is justified by the fact that it indicates how the sentence should be interpreted. Purely emotional underlining should be avoided.

published in 1875.   In March, 1876, he testified against the War Department's
Indian policy, thus angering President Grant.[5]   Few Americans in 1876 were

23 better known than Custer.   Yet he was more than a famous person; he was a

24 scapegoat.   Americans who felt secretly ashamed of the mistreatment of Indians
may have felt that the entire nation was responsible for Custer's death; this
attitude is suggested today by the book and song title and bumper sticker,
Custer Died for Your Sins.   Perhaps, however, he was even more than a victim;
he was a tragic figure.   Without realizing it, a hero in classical tragedy
brings about his own downfall.   In 1874 Custer's expedition into the Black Hills

25 had attracted miners and helped stir up the Sioux.   Furthermore, in 1875 Custer
and his brother had jailed Rain-in-the-Face, who, many believed, led the Sioux
rebellion.[6]   Finally, Custer's impetuous thirst for battle and his division of
his forces contributed to his defeat.   His partial responsibility for his own
fate probably stirred people's emotions.

26   Other aspects of Custer's defeat carried emotional appeal.   Killed with
Custer were two of his brothers, a brother-in-law, and a nephew.   The grief of
Mrs. Custer stirred the nation's sympathy.   The alleged mutilation of the
bodies by Sioux squaws added a gruesome touch.   In a letter to the Helena

27 Daily Herald, Lieutenant James H. Bradley, who discovered the bodies, denied

28 that many were mutilated,[7] but Indian experts all over the nation refuted him.

29 In the legend the bodies had to be mutilated.   Stories of the subsequent fate
of the bodies persisted for years.   General Terry's men buried the officers in
shallow graves but left many enlisted men unburied.   A year later, a military
detail found many skeletons uncovered.   Custer's remains were sent to West
Point for reburial.   In 1885 all bones found on the surface were buried in a
mass grave at the base of a monument.   Markers were later set up by guesswork;

30 Up to this point, the paper contains an average number of citation notes. There are considerably more in the rest of the paper because of the necessity of citing details related to the legend.

31 In this sentence and the two following sentences, note the blending of quoted material with the text.

32 quotation

Holbrook, p. 235   survivor

Silent Smith

"Where was I? I was lying under a hoss, wounded but much alive, and I had lain there for two days."

found horse in saloon painting

33 Obviously, the dead horse is used as a link between the survivor stories and Comanche. Sometimes material can be arranged so that a detail will serve as a stepping-stone to the next unit in the plan.

34 The closing phrase relates the Comanche story to the thesis.

a small patch of thick grass indicated that a man's body had enriched the soil,
but large patches were assumed to represent resting places of horses.[8] News
stories about the bodies kept Custer's name before the public. Claims of
survivors also kept the legend alive. According to Lawrence A. Frost, over 200
30 men turned up at various times claiming to have survived the battle.[9] The
most famous was Curly, one of Custer's Indian scouts; he probably left before
the fight began, but in the legend he escaped by wearing a Sioux blanket.[10]
Why the Sioux wore blankets on a hot June day is never explained. Frederick
Whittaker, an author of dime novels who published a long biography of Custer in
31 1876, described Curly urging Custer to flee with him: Custer "looked at Curly,
waved him away and rode back to his little group of men, to die with them."[11]
A later biographer improved on this story: Curly "made himself up to resemble
a Sioux" and urged Custer to do the same, but "the General scorned to do it."[12]
32 Stewart H. Holbrook described another survivor, a talkative old man nicknamed
Silent Smith, who explained his escape very simply: "Where was I? I was lying
under a hoss, wounded but much alive, and I had lain there for two days."
After drinking the free beer earned by his story, Silent Smith inspected a
33 painting of the battle and identified the very horse that saved his life.[13]
Actually, the only survivor was a live horse. Comanche, the mount of Captain
Miles Keogh, was found on the field wounded in seven places. He was suspended
in a sling for a year while his wounds were treated. After recovering he was
made an honorary member of the Seventh Cavalry; draped in black with reversed
boots in the stirrups, he was led in all regimental parades. After Comanche
died in 1891, his body was stuffed; it is now on exhibition in a museum of the
34 University of Kansas[14]-- a picturesque reminder of the Custer legend.

Because many questions arose concerning Custer's defeat that could not be

35 The introductory clauses in the topic sentence recall the last two subdivisions of the previous paragraph. The paragraph is developed in three stages. A controversy would ordinarily divide into two subtopics, pro and con. However, since the student found some defenders of the army in general and some of Custer in particular, it seemed advisable to discuss each separately. Some opinions of military men, which would have complicated the plan unduly, are included in an explanation note (n. 15).

36 quotation reduced to a summary

Miller, p. 204   *defenders*

"Custer was known to have been an excellent tactician by all existing standards. An excuse for his defeat at the hands of mere savages must somehow be devised. Among the propounders of the legend, certain graduates of West Point between 1846 and 1850 recalled a cadet of unusual appearance nicknamed Bison. . . . Bison's age and description — even his sallow skin — came close to matching that of Custer's archfoe, Sitting Bull. At once the authorities circulated a rumor to the effect that Sitting Bull had acquired a superior knowledge of strategy at West Point."

---

37 The defenders of Custer are discussed in chronological order.

38 Note the blending of quotations with the student's sentences.

39 The phrase "To accuse Benteen of malice and Reno of cowardice," an echo of the quotation, serves as a transition to the third subtopic (Reno).

40 The quotation marks around "whitewashing" suggest that the term verges on slang and, more importantly, look ahead to its use in the headline that follows.

41 A quotation of four lines or more is written in block or display form. A shorter passage may sometimes be written in this way to give it special emphasis. A block quotation is indented ten spaces and single-spaced; no quotation marks are used unless they appear in the source. This quotation is centered because it is a simulated headline. Block quotations are convenient and economical, but they should not be overused. A good paper does not often quote long passages, and many readers are inclined to skip them.

    Block quotations are double-spaced in a manuscript that is to be printed. If this procedure is followed, notes and bibliography entries of more than one line should also be double-spaced—an unnecessary waste of space in a student paper.

35 answered by any living person, the battle has been the subject of controversy.[15]

Admirers of the army, who could not accept the defeat of crack cavalry troops

by Indians, invented some bizarre explanations, including a theory that a dark-

36 skinned cadet at West Point from 1846 to 1850 was actually Sitting Bull.[16]

Some hinted that former Confederate officers planned the Indian strategy. A

more sensible reason was that Custer's men carried defective carbines that jammed

37 after being fired two or three times.[17] Custer's partisans were numerous.

Frederick Whittaker blamed Reno for not riding to rescue his commander. Mrs.

38 Custer wrote that her husband "fought against terrible odds, expecting momen-

tarily to be joined by the other portions of the regiment, that were then in

retreat."[18] With less restraint a later admirer of Custer described the moment

when Benteen joined Reno, who "was a sworn enemy of the man fighting on the bluffs

to the north. Benteen, blinded by hate, dismounted his troopers. Reno, shaken

with fear, raised his pistol and fired at an Indian a thousand yards away."[19]

39 To accuse Benteen of malice and Reno of cowardice has been the common practice of

Custer's supporters. Reno was the chief scapegoat. In 1879 he demanded a court

of inquiry. Twenty-three witnesses were examined in hearings that lasted four

weeks. The finding of the court was that "while subordinates in some instances

did more for the safety of the command . . . than did Major Reno, there was

40 nothing in his conduct which requires animadversion from this court."[20] This

"whitewashing" of Reno infuriated Whittaker, who sent a long letter to the New

York Sun attacking Reno in terms that the headline suggests:

GEN. CUSTER AND MAJ. RENO

One Who Died at the Little Big Horn and
One Who Ran Away
41 Enemies Wracking [sic] their Spite on a
Hero's Memory . . .
A Whitewashing Court of Inquiry[21]

42   *The subject of the sentence, "verdict," is a transitional echo of the previous paragraph.*

43   *The paragraph is organized in three subtopics: movies, paintings, and poems. Poems are discussed last because a poem provides a transition to the closing paragraph (see p. 9.)*

44   *Custer has been portrayed in more than twenty movies, but merely listing the titles would serve no useful purpose. Three examples are used to illustrate the variety of opinions about his character.*

45   *Note the clarifying details within brackets and the ellipsis indicating that words have been omitted.*

46   *The year within the student's sentence is enclosed in parentheses rather than brackets.*

47   *part of a quotation (ellipsis unnecessary)*

Fenin, p. 370   movie - <u>LBM</u>

"Penn uses the film to express his personal philosophy with vigor, saving his most passionate feeling for describing past horrors reminiscent of present ones. His excoriation of George Armstrong Custer is one of the most pitiless indictments of a pompous fool ever witnessed on a screen."

---

48   *A discussion of all paintings of the battle would require a paper in itself. The second subtopic, therefore, mentions two early paintings and makes general reference to others.*

49   *The cluster of notes here is unusually large, but numerous citations are needed because of the point-by-point contrast between paintings and the historical record. Note that generalized references are not cited. The student supposedly has seen several reproductions and does not need to document each detail that appears in a picture. Similarly, the sentence regarding Custer's death is not cited. No authority is needed for the supposition that he may have died early in the battle.*

50   *The names of paintings are usually underlined, but quotation marks are not incorrect. This title is in quotation marks because it is not the actual name of the painting.*

42   The verdict of the court of inquiry, naturally, did not close the

43 controversy. In both factual and imaginative accounts, there are contradictions

44 that seem typical of a legend. Custer has been a favorite subject of movie

producers. Two films made at almost the same time illustrate the range of

variations in conceptions of his character:

45

> In _Santa Fe Trail_ [1940], played by Ronald Reagan, he was a
> quiet, sincere, and dedicated soldier; as written for Errol
> Flynn [_They Died With Their Boots On_, 1941] he became the
> embodiment of the daredevil soldier, contemptuous of orders.
> . . . Later, of course, according to this particular script, he
> became something of an idealist.[22]

46 In _Little Big Man_ (1970), Custer is raving mad during the battle; this

47 portrayal of Custer has been described as "one of the most pitiless indictments

of a pompous fool ever witnessed on a screen."[23] According to Lawrence A.

48 Frost, there have been more than 1000 paintings of the battle.[24] The first

49 picture was drawn by A. K. Waud for Whittaker's life of Custer.[25] The most

famous was painted in 1888 by Cassily Adams; he depicted the battle scene on

a canvas wagon cover sixteen feet long and nine feet high. It was displayed

in a St. Louis saloon, where it aroused the admiration of a brewer, Adolphus

Busch, who had lithographs made. Over 250,000 copies were distributed, and

50 the "Anheuser-Busch Last Stand" hung in many western barrooms.[26] All paintings

of the battle differ from each other and from known facts. Custer is often

shown with his long hair blowing in the breeze, but his hair was clipped short

before the expedition began. He is often pictured in full-dress uniform;

actually, he wore a blue shirt and buckskin breeches.[27] Sometimes he is shown

impaled by several arrows, but he was killed by rifle wounds in the breast and

the left temple.[28] He is shown fighting with a saber, sometimes astride a

plunging horse. According to General Edward S. Godfrey, sabers were not worn;

51   *Sources used by the student cite opinions of others, General Godfrey (p.8) and Chief Gall. By identifying them in the text and citing the sources in notes, the student has simplified the documentation.*

52   *quotation reduced to a summary*

Utley, p. 108   horse – holders

Chief Gall at 10ᵗʰ anniversary of battle

"' The warriors directed a special fire against the troops who held the horses,' he said, ' and as soon as the holder was hit, by waving blankets and great shouting the horses were stampeded, which made it impossible for the soldiers to escape.'"

---

53   *The transition to the third subtopic (poems) is accomplished by a comparison ("as diverse").*

54   *Both Longfellow and Whittaker have been mentioned earlier. Used sparingly, recurring details reinforce the coherence of a paper.*

55   *The title of a poem not published as a separate unit is enclosed in quotation marks.*

56   *Poetry of more than two lines is written in block form.*

57   *The transition to the final paragraph is accomplished by a play on words. The phrase "last words" is repeated in a different sense in the topic sentence of the new paragraph.*

58   *The purpose of the concluding paragraph is to summarize the main ideas of the essay in terms of the thesis. The second sentence recapitulates the main topics of the second section of the outline (II. The legend) more neatly than is usually possible.*

59   *Since the closing paragraph summarizes what has been said in the paper and presents no totally new ideas, it is not shown in the outline. A separate concluding paragraph is not always necessary. Sometimes a paper can close with an especially vivid detail or quotation; more often a summarizing sentence can be used at the close of the last main paragraph.*

51 Custer carried a knife, two pistols, and a sporting rifle.[29] According to

52 Chief Gall, a Sioux leader, the troopers dismounted to fight and the Indians directed their fire against the men holding the horses.[30] Custer is often

shown surrounded by dying troopers, but he may have been killed early in the

53 fight. Poetic versions are as diverse as the paintings. Many poets besides

54 Longfellow published laments for Custer. Whittier, the Quaker poet, wrote "On

55 the Little Big Horn," calling for peace between the red man and the white.

John Hay wrote a tribute to Comanche, "Miles Keogh's Horse." Whittaker,

Custer's aggressive biographer, wrote "Custer's Last Charge," in which he

quoted his hero's last words:

56

> Closer and closer the death circle growing.
> Ever the leader's voice, clarion clear,
> Rang out his words of encouragement glowing,
> "We can die but once, boys, -- we'll sell out lives dear!"[31]

57   The last words of the legend-makers will never be spoken. The impact with

58 which the news hit the country, the flamboyant personality of Custer, the grief and horror the tragedy evoked, the bitter debate over the record, and the

imaginative versions of the fight combine to keep it fresh in American minds.

His long yellow hair whipping in the wind, his dress uniform spotless and

unwrinkled, arrows protruding from his chest, his saber brandished in his left

hand, his troopers sprawled in death around him, Custer calmly draws a bead on

the galloping Sioux encircling him. This scene in all its wild inaccuracy is

59 a permanent legend in American folklore.

The form of each note is identified briefly along with any special features.

1 Standard primary form

2 Primary form, revised edition

3 Joint authors, citation of fifteen pages that are summarized, separate citation of quoted material

4 Secondary citation using a short title

5 Article in a standard reference work. The publisher is omitted as is done with encyclopedias. Because the work is alphabetically arranged, the volume and page are not strictly necessary.

6 An explanation and reference note. Two lines of poetry are usually written continuously and separated by a slash with one space before and after.

7 Standard primary form. The words "Publishing Co." would ordinarily be omitted, but omitting them here might result in confusion.

8 Primary form for a book with no author

9 Secondary citation, a split note since the author is identified in the text

10 Standard primary form

11 Double reference, the original source followed by a standard primary citation of the source quoted in the paper

12 Standard primary form

13 A monthly magazine, a split note since the author is identified in the text

14 Secondary citation of the book cited in n. 11

Notes

[1] Lawrence A. Frost, <u>Custer Legends</u> (Bowling Green, Ohio: Bowling Green Univ. Popular Press, 1981), p. 7.

[2] E. A. Brininstool, <u>Troopers with Custer</u>, rev. ed. (Harrisburg, Pa.: Stackpool, 1952), pp. 5-11.

[3] Edward S. Luce and Evelyn S. Luce, <u>Custer Battlefield National Monument, Montana</u> (Washington, D.C.: National Park Service, 1952), pp. 9-23. Cooke's message is printed on p. 18 and is pictured on p. 22.

[4] Brininstool, <u>Troopers</u>, pp. 251-54.

[5] "Custer, George Armstrong," <u>DAB</u> (1930), vol. 5, pp. 7-9.

[6] Rain-in-the-Face, it was reported, swore to eat Tom Custer's heart. For a poem by Longfellow entitled "The Revenge of Rain-in-the-Face," see Burton. E. Stevenson, ed. <u>Poems of American History</u>, rev. ed. (Boston: Houghton Mifflin, 1922), pp. 583-84. The poem describes the chief riding off with "The brave heart, that beat no more, / Of the White Chief with yellow hair." Longfellow's confusing Custer with his brother is typical of the way events are distorted in the growth of a legend.

[7] W. A. Graham, <u>The Story of the Little Big Horn</u> (Harrisburg, Pa.: Military Service Publishing Co., 1952), p. 166.

[8] <u>Montana</u> (New York: Hastings House, 1949), p. 263.

[9] <u>Custer Legends</u>, p. 213.

[10] David Humphreys Miller, <u>Custer's Fall</u> (New York: Duell, Sloan and Pearce, 1957), p. 202.

[11] <u>A Complete Life of Gen. George A. Custer</u> (New York, 1876), p. 599, quoted in Robert M. Utley, <u>Custer and the Great Controversy</u> (Los Angeles: Westernlore Press, 1962), p. 123.

[12] F. S. Dellenbaugh, <u>George Armstrong Custer</u> (New York: Macmillan, 1917), p. 184.

[13] "Phonies of the Old West," <u>American Mercury</u>, Feb. 1949, p. 235.

[14] Utley, <u>Controversy</u>, pp. 143-45.

15 An explanation note containing material that did not fit the paragraph plan, secondary citations. The author and title are not necessary in the second and third citations because the context makes the source obvious.

16 Secondary citation

17 Standard primary form. The state is abbreviated after the city but not in the name of the press.

18 A split note, the author identified in the text

19 Standard primary form

20 Secondary citation

21 Standard primary form followed by an explanation note that includes a citation of a newspaper

22 Joint authors, a revised edition

23 Secondary citation. Because short titles are necessary for the two books by W. A. Graham, they are used for all books, but it would not be wrong to omit the title when the source is as obvious as it is here.

24 Secondary citation, a split note, the author identified in the text

25 Secondary citation

26 Secondary citation. The small Roman numerals indicate material from the preface.

27 Secondary citation

28 Secondary citation

29 Secondary citation

30 Secondary citation

31 Secondary citation followed by a comment and a secondary citation

[15] Many military men involved themselves in the dispute over Custer's tactics. President Grant told a reporter that the defeat was "a sacrifice of troops, brought on by Custer himself" (Utley, Controversy, p. 44). General Samuel D. Sturgis, commanding officer of the Seventh Cavalry though on detached service, said that Custer "made his attack recklessly, earlier by thirty-six hours than he should have done, and with men tired out from forced marches" (p. 45). General Thomas L Rosser, a former Confederate officer, defended Custer and blamed the defeat on Reno, "who took to the hills, and abandoned Custer and his gallant comrades to their fate" (p. 47).

[16] Miller, Custer's Fall, p. 204.

[17] Edgar I. Stewart, Custer's Luck (Norman, Okla.: Univ. of Oklahoma Press, 1966), p. 458.

[18] Tenting on the Plains or General Custer in Kansas and Texas (New York: C. L. Webster, 1887), p. 21.

[19] Frazier Hunt, Custer, the Last of the Cavaliers (New York: Cosmopolitan, 1928), p. 2.

[20] Utley, Controversy, pp. 59-62.

[21] W. A. Graham, The Custer Myth (Harrisburg, Pa.: Stackpole, 1953), p. 326. In 1967 a grandnephew of Major Reno asked the Army to clear his name and order his reburial at Custer Battlefield National Cemetery. The record was reviewed, and Major Reno was reburied at the battlefield on 9 Sept. 1967 (New York Times, 10 Sept. 1967, Sec. 1, p. 41).

[22] George N. Fenin and William K. Everson, The Western from Silents to the Seventies, rev. ed. (New York: Grossman, 1973), pp. 11-12.

[23] Fenin and Everson, The Western, p. 370.

[24] Custer Legends, p. 3.

[25] Reproduced in Graham, Myth, p. 17.

[26] Graham, Story, p. xi.

[27] Graham, Myth, p. xiii.

[28] Stewart, Custer's Luck, p. 471.

[29] Graham, Myth, pp. 345-46.

[30] Utley, Controversy, p. 108.

[31] Stevenson, ed., Poems, p. 582. According to General Godfrey, Sitting Bull, a medicine man and not a warrior, took no active part in the battle (Graham, Myth, p. 13).

The form of each entry is identified briefly.

Brininstool revised edition of a book with a subtitle. Subtitles are omitted in notes.

Custer a standard book entry

"Custer" an article in a standard reference that is alphabetically arranged. Only the year is strictly necessary; volume and pages are cited in the note.

Dellenbaugh a standard book entry

Fenin joint authors. Note that second name is not inverted.

Frost a standard book entry

Graham a standard book entry, subtitle

_____ a standard book entry, subtitle. A line of ten spaces denotes a second work by the same author.

Holbrook a monthly magazine. Volume numbers are indicated only for quarterlies.

Hunt a standard book entry with identification of the illustrator

Luce joint authors. The name of a series is not underlined.

Miller a standard book entry, subtitle

Montana a book in a series, no author

New an unsigned news story

Stevenson an edited work, revised edition. The editor is cited first to avoid "Rev. ed. ed."

Bibliography

Brininstool, E. A. Troopers with Custer: Historic Events of the Battle of the Little Big Horn. Rev. ed. Harrisburg, Pa.: Stackpole, 1952.

Custer, Elizabeth B. Tenting on the Plains or General Custer in Kansas and Texas. New York: C. L. Webster, 1887.

"Custer, George Armstrong." Dictionary of American Biography. New York: Scribner's, 1930.

Dellenbaugh, Frederick S. George Armstrong Custer. New York: Macmillan, 1917.

Fenin, George N., and William K. Everson. The Western from Silents to the Seventies. Rev. ed. New York: Grossman, 1973.

Frost, Lawrence A. Custer Legends. Bowling Green, Ohio: Bowling Greem Univ. Popular Press, 1981.

Graham, W. A. The Custer Myth: A Source Book of Custeriana. Harrisburg, Pa.: Stackpole, 1953.

_____. The Story of the Little Big Horn: Custer's Last Fight. Harrisburg, Pa.: Military Service Publishing Co., 1952.

Holbrook, Stewart H. "Phonies of the Old West." American Mercury, Feb. 1949, pp. 230-35.

Hunt, Frazier. Custer, The Last of the Cavaliers. Illus. Captain John W. Thomason. New York: Cosmopolitan, 1928.

Luce, Edward S., and Evelyn S. Luce. Custer Battlefield National Monument, Montana. National Park Service Historical Handbook Series. Washington, D.C.: National Park Service, 1952.

Miller, David Humphreys. Custer's Fall: The Indian Side of the Story. New York: Duell, Sloan and Pearce, 1957.

Montana. American Guide Series. New York: Hastings House, 1949.

New York Times, 10 Sept. 1967, Sec. 1, p. 41.

Stevenson, Burton E., ed. Poems of American History. Rev. ed. Boston: Houghton Mifflin, 1922.

Stewart standard primary form

Utley standard primary form, subtitle, series

Stewart, Edgar I. Custer's Luck. Norman, Okla.: Univ. of Oklahoma Pess, 1966.

Utley, Robert M. Custer and the Great Controversy: Origin and Development of
    a Legend. Great West and Indian Series. Los Angeles: Westernlore Press,
    1962.

FOOTNOTES

Endnotes are now used more often than footnotes in student papers. As the facing page demonstrates, footnotes and endnotes are identical in form.

Quadruple-space between the last line of the text and the first footnote. A line fifteen spaces long or a line across the page can also be used, but the extra space should be adequate separation.

Unless your instructor specifies double-spacing throughout, single-space each note and double-space between notes.

a small patch of thick grass indicated that a man's body had enriched the soil, but large patches were assumed to represent resting places of horses.[8] News stories about the bodies kept Custer's name before the public. Claims of survivors also kept the legend alive. According to Lawrence A. Frost, over 200 men turned up at various times claiming to have survived the battle.[9] The most famous was Curly, one of Custer's Indian scouts; he probably left before the fight began, but in the legend he escaped by wearing a Sioux blanket.[10] Why the Sioux wore blankets on a hot June day is never explained. Frederick Whittaker, an author of dime novels who published a long biography of Custer in 1876, described Curly urging Custer to flee with him: Custer "looked at Curly, waved him away and rode back to his little group of men, to die with them."[11] F. S. Dellenbaugh, a later biographer, improved on this story: Curly "made himself up to resemble a Sioux" and urged Custer to do the same, but "the General scorned to do it."[12] Stewart H. Holbrook described another survivor, a talkative old man nicknamed Silent Smith, who explained his escape very simply: "Where was I? I was lying under a hoss, wounded but much alive, and I had lain there for two days." After drinking the free beer earned by his story, Silent Smith inspected a painting of the battle and identified the very

[8] _Montana_ (New York: Hastings House, 1949), p. 263.

[9] _Custer Legends_, p. 213.

[10] David Humpreys Miller, _Custer's Fall_ (New York: Duell, Sloan and Pearce, 1957), p. 202.

[11] _A Complete Life of Gen. George A. Custer_ (New York, 1876), p. 599, quoted in Robert M. Utley, _Custer and the Great Controversy_ (Los Angeles: Westernlore Press, 1962), p. 123.

[12] F. S. Dellenbaugh, _George Armstrong Custer_ (New York: Macmillan, 1917), p. 184.

SAMPLE RESEARCH PAPER
New MLA Style

The two versions of the sample paper are identical in content. The following version, documented in the new MLA style, requires only three endnotes containing explanatory comment. All other citation is internal. The 1984 MLA Handbook recommends a somewhat different format from that generally used in the past. Each page is numbered in the upper right corner a half inch from the top of the page. There should be margins of one inch on both sides and at the bottom. A paragraph is indented five spaces. A block or display quotation is indented ten spaces. The citation in parentheses is not followed by a period. The closing parenthesis should be flush with the right margin of the quotation, on the same line if there is room for it or two spaces down if necessary.

On the first page of your paper, you should type on separate lines on the left margin your name, your instructor's name, your course number, and the date. Double-space and type the title, centered on the page. Double-space twice and begin the text of your paper.

George Spelvin
Professor Wright
English 101H
27 April 1984

The Custer Legend

All Americans have heard of Custer's Last Stand. Many cherish a romantic
but inaccurate vision of George Armstrong Custer wielding his saber against the
onrushing Sioux. The battle has been described many times, and more has been
written about Custer than any American except Washington and Lincoln (Frost 7).
Both the battle and Custer himself are familiar because they are legends. A
legend develops because of a wide range of imaginative and emotional appeals.

The Custer legend began as a simple maneuver in a large-scale operation.
The plan called for three columns to converge on the Sioux, who had left their
reservations. A column from the west under Colonel John Gibbon was to start
from Fort Ellis, Montana, and a column under General George Crook was to
advance from the south. General Crook encountered Sioux on the Rosebud River
and was forced to withdraw after a fierce fight. Neither Custer nor his
commander, General Alfred H. Terry, knew about this battle. Their column,
commanded by General Terry, left Fort Abraham Lincoln, Dakota Territory, on
May 17, 1876. Where the Rosebud empties into the Yellowstone River, Terry
joined Gibbon's column. Terry ordered Gibbon to march south along the Little
Big Horn. Custer was to follow the Rosebud, swing west, and march north along
the Little Big Horn. The Sioux would thus be caught between the two forces.
Terry accompanied Gibbon's forces (Brininstool 5-11). Custer was on his own.

Free of the supervision of his commander, Custer apparently sought battle

1

as speedily as possible. He twice divided his forces. On June 25, though warned by his scouts that a Sioux village lay ahead, he sent Captain F. W. Benteen to the left with three troops. One troop brought up the rear with the packs. Three troops were assigned to Major M. A. Reno. The remaining five troops were under Custer himself. Benteen's party was soon hidden by high bluffs and cottonwood trees. After about two hours Custer again divided his force, sending Reno across the river. Reno attacked the Sioux village and after hard fighting withdrew to the eastern bank. He took refuge on high ground, where he was later joined by Benteen. They were pinned down and knew

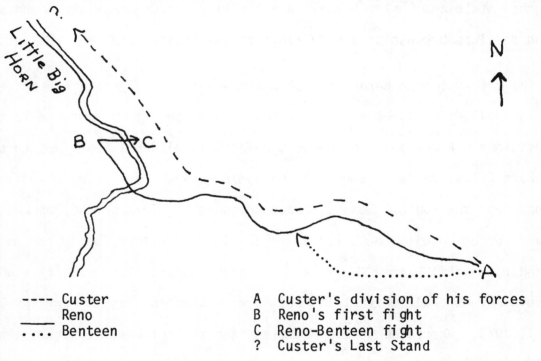

```
---- Custer        A  Custer's division of his forces
____ Reno          B  Reno's first fight
.... Benteen       C  Reno-Benteen fight
                   ?  Custer's Last Stand
```

Based on Edward S. Luce and Evelyn S. Luce, Custer Battlefield National Monument, Montana (Washington, DC: National Park Service, 1952). 13.

nothing of Custer's fate until Gibbon reached them on June 27. Custer had been lost from sight before Reno's troops charged. He had veered to the right, perhaps to attack the village from another direction. Soon he must have realized that his scouts had been correct. A hastily scribbled note was sent

by courier: "Benteen -- Come on -- Big village -- Be quick -- Bring packs.
W. W. Cooke [Custer's adjutant]. P.S. Bring pacs [sic]." The message to
Benteen is the last verifiable word from Custer. His entire command was wiped
out. The bodies were discovered on June 27 by Gibbon's men (Luce 9-23, for
text of message see 18). With Custer's futile appeal to Benteen, fact stops
and legend begins.

From the beginning the Custer story seemed destined to become a legend.
Even the way the news broke was spectacular. News of the battle did not reach
the outside world until July 4. A scout named Taylor carried the news from
the battlefield. Accounts differ, but in one of the most impressive, a rancher
named Horace Countryman rode 180 miles with only one change of horses to reach
Helena, Montana, with Taylor's story. Such a heroic exploit suits a legend.
Andrew J. Fisk, editor of the Helena Daily Herald, rounded up enough
celebrating printers to issue a special edition (Brininstool 251-54).
Eastern newspapers carried the story on July 6. In Washington and Philadelphia
the centennial of independence had just been celebrated. To a nation still in
a holiday mood, the catastrophe must have been a stunning shock. Many people
probably remembered the Custer defeat all their lives because of the ironic
coincidence of its occurring just before the Centennial Fourth of July.

The shock of the news was also intensified by Custer's celebrity. He had
been in the public eye for nearly fifteen years. After graduating at the
bottom of his West Point class in 1861, he attracted the attention of several
ranking officers and advanced rapidly. As a temporary major general, known
for his colorful uniforms and long blond hair, he led the pursuit of Lee's army
in the last days of the Civil War and received the first flag of truce. In
1868 he defeated a band of Cheyennes at the Battle of Washita. His exploration

of the Black Hills in 1874 inspired a gold rush. Frontier sketches that he wrote for The Galaxy made up a best-selling book, My Life on the Plains, published in 1875. In March, 1876, he testified against the War Department's Indian policy, thus angering President Grant (DAB 5: 7-9). Few Americans in 1876 were better known than Custer. Yet he was more than a famous person; he was a scapegoat. Americans who felt secretly ashamed of the mistreatment of Indians may have felt that the entire nation was responsible for Custer's death; this attitude is suggested today by the book and song title and bumper sticker, Custer Died for Your Sins. Perhaps, however, he was even more than a victim; he was a tragic figure. Without realizing it, a hero in classical tragedy brings about his own downfall. In 1874 Custer's expedition into the Black Hills had attracted miners and helped stir up the Sioux. Furthermore, in 1875 Custer and his brother had jailed Rain-in-the-Face, who, many believed, led the Sioux rebellion.[1] Finally, Custer's impetuous thirst for battle and his division of his forces contributed to his defeat. His partial responsibility for his own fate probably stirred people's emotions.

Other aspects of Custer's defeat carried emotional appeal. Killed with Custer were two of his brothers, a brother-in-law, and a nephew. The grief of Mrs. Custer stirred the nation's sympathy. The alleged mutilation of the bodies by Sioux squaws added a gruesome touch. In a letter to the Helena Daily Herald, Lieutentant James H. Bradley, who discovered the bodies, denied that many were mutilated (Graham, Story 166), but Indian experts all over the nation refuted him. In the legend the bodies had to be mutilated. Stories of the subsequent fate of the bodies persisted for years. General Terry's men buried the officers in shallow graves but left many enlisted men unburied. A year later, a military detail found many skeletons uncovered. Custer's remains were sent to West Point for reburial. In 1885 all bones found on the surface were buried in a mass grave at the base of a monument. Markers were later set up by guesswork; a small patch of thick grass indicated that man's body had enriched the soil, but large patches were assumed to represent resting places for horses (Montana 263). News stories about the bodies kept Custer's name before the public. Claims of survivors also kept the legend alive. According to Lawrence A. Frost, over 200 men turned up at various times claiming to have survived the battle (213). The most famous was Curly, one of Custer's Indian scouts; he probably left before the fight began, but in the legend he escaped by wearing a Sioux blanket (Miller 202). Why the Sioux wore blankets on a hot June day is never explained. Frederick Whittaker, an author of dime novels who published a long biography of Custer in 1876, described Curly urging Custer to flee with him: Custer "looked at Curly, waved him away and rode back to his little group of men, to die with them" (599 qtd. in Utley 123). F. S. Dellen-baugh, a later biographer, improved on this story: Curly "made himself up to resemble a Sioux" and urged Custer to do the same, but "the General scorned to do it" (184). Stewart H. Holbrook described another survivor, a talkative old man nicknamed Silent Smith, who explained his escape very simply: "Where was I? I was lying under a hoss, wounded but much alive, and I had lain there for two days." After drinking the free beer earned by his story, Silent Smith inspected a painting of the battle and identified the very horse that saved his life (235). Actually, the only survivor was a live horse. Comanche, the mount of Captain Miles Keogh, was found on the field wounded in seven places. He was suspended in a sling for a year while his wounds were treated. After recovering he was made an honorary member of the Seventh Cavalry; draped in black with reversed boots in the stirrups, he was led in all regimental parades. After Comanche died in 1891, his body was stuffed; it is now on exhibition in a museum of the University of Kansas (Utley 143-45) -- a picturesque reminder of the Custer legend.

Because many questions arose concerning Custer's defeat that could not be answered by any living person, the battle has been the subject of controversy.[2] Admirers of the army, who could not accept the defeat of crack cavalry troops by Indians, invented some bizarre explanations, including a theory that a dark-skinned cadet at West Point from 1846 to 1850 was actually Sitting Bull (Miller 204). Some hinted that former Confederate officers planned the Indian strategy. A more sensible reason was that Custer's men carried defective carbines that jammed after being fired two or three times (Stewart 458). Custer's partisans were numerous. Frederick Whittaker blamed Reno for not riding to rescue his commander. Mrs. Custer wrote that her husband "fought against terrible odds, expecting momentarily to be joined by the other portions of the regiment, that were then in retreat" (21). With less restraint a later admirer of Custer described the moment when Benteen joined Reno, who "was a sworn enemy of the man fighting on the bluffs to the north. Benteen, blinded by hate, dismounted his troopers. Reno, shaken with fear, raised his pistol and fired at an Indian a thousand yards away" (Hunt 2). To accuse Benteen of malice and Reno of cowardice has been the common practice of Custer's supporters. Reno was the chief scapegoat. In 1879 he demanded a court of inquiry. Twenty-three witnesses were examined in hearings that lasted four weeks. The finding of the court was that "while subordinates in some instances did more for the safety of the command . . . than did Major Reno, there was nothing in his conduct which requires animadversion from this court" (Utley 59-62). This "whitewashing" of Reno infuriated Whittaker, who sent a long letter to the New York Sun attacking Reno in terms that the headline suggests:

GEN. CUSTER AND MAJ. RENO

One Who Died at the Little Big Horn and

One Who Ran Away

Enemies Wracking [sic] their Spite on a

Hero's Memory . . .

A Whitewashing Court of Inquiry (Graham, Myth 326)[3]

The verdict of the court of inquiry, naturally, did not close the controversy. In both factual and imaginative accounts, there are contradictions that seem typical of a legend. Custer has been a favorite subject of movie producers. Two films made at almost the same time illustrate the range of variations in conceptions of his character:

> In Santa Fe Trail [1940], played by Ronald Reagan, he was a
> quiet, sincere, and dedicated soldier; as written for Errol
> Flynn [They Died With Their Boots On, 1941] he became the
> embodiment of the daredevil soldier, contemptuous of orders.
> . . . Later, of course, according to this particular script,
> he became something of an idealist. (Fenin and Everson 11-12)

In Little Big Man (1970), Custer is raving mad during the battle; this portrayal of Custer has been described as "one of the most pitiless indictments of a pompous fool ever witnessed on the screen" (Fenin and Everson 370). According to Lawrence A. Frost, there have been more than 1000 paintings of the battle (3). The first picture was drawn by A. K. Waud for Whittaker's life of Custer (reproduced in Graham, Myth 17). The most famous was painted in 1888 by Cassily Adams; he depicted the battle scene on a canvas wagon cover sixteen feet long and nine feet high. It was displayed in a St. Louis saloon, where it aroused the admiration of a brewer, Adolphus Busch, who had lithographs

made. Over 250,000 copies were distributed, and the "Anheuser-Busch Last
Stand" hung in many western barrooms (Graham, Story xi). All paintings of the
battle differ from each other and from known facts. Custer is often shown with
his long hair blowing in the breeze, but his hair was clipped short before the
expedition began. He is often pictured in full-dress uniform; actually, he
wore a blue shirt and buckskin breeches (Graham, Myth xiii). Sometimes he is
shown impaled by several arrows, but he was killed by rifle wounds in the
breast and the left temple (Stewart 471). He is shown fighting with a saber,
sometimes astride a plunging horse. According to General Edward S. Godfrey,
sabers were not worn; Custer carried a knife, two pistols, and a sporting rifle
(Graham, Myth 345-46). According to Chief Gall, a Sioux leader, the troopers
dismounted to fight, and the Indians directed their fire against the men
holding the horses (Utley 108). Custer is often shown surrounded by dying
troopers, but he may have been killed early in the fight. Poetic versions are
as diverse as the paintings. Many poets besides Longfellow published laments
for Custer. Whittier, the Quaker poet, wrote "On the Little Big Horn," calling
for peace between the red man and the white. John Hay wrote a tribute to
Comanche, "Miles Keogh's Horse." Whittaker, Custer's aggressive biographer,
wrote "Custer's Last Charge," in which he even quoted his hero's last words:

> Closer and closer the death circle growing,
>
> Ever the leader's voice, clarion clear,
>
> Rang out his words of encouragement glowing,
>
> "We can die but once, boys, -- we'll sell our lives dear!"
>
> (Stevenson 582)

The last words of the legend-makers will never be spoken. The impact with
which the news hit the country, the flamboyant personality of Custer, the grief

and horror the tragedy evoked, the bitter debate over the record, and the imaginative versions of the fight combine to keep it fresh in American minds. His long yellow hair whipping in the wind, his dress uniform spotless and unwrinkled, arrows protruding from his chest, his saber brandished in his left hand, his troopers sprawled in death around him, Custer calmly draws a bead on the galloping Sioux encircling him. This scene in all its wild inaccuracy is a permanent legend in American folklore.

Notes

[1] Rain-in-the-Face, it was reported, swore to eat Tom Custer's heart.
For a poem by Longfellow entitled "The Revenge of Rain-in-the-Face," see
Stevenson 583-84. The poem describes the chief riding off with "The brave
heart, that beat no more, / Of the White Chief with yellow hair." Longfellow's
confusing Custer with his brother is typical of the way events are distorted in
the growth of a legend.

[2] Many military men involved themselves in the dispute over Custer's
tactics. President Grant told a reporter that the defeat was "a sacrifice of
troops, brought on by Custer himself" (Utley 44). General Samuel D. Sturgis,
commanding officer of the Seventh Cavalry though on detached service, said that
Custer "made his attack recklessly, earlier by thirty-six hours than he should
have done, and with men tired out from forced marches" (45). General Thomas L.
Rosser, a former Confederate officer, defended Custer and blamed the defeat on
Reno, "who took to the hills, and abandoned Custer and his gallant comrades to
their fate" (47).

[3] In 1967 a grandnephew of Major Reno asked the Army to clear his name
and order his reburial at Custer Battlefield National Cemetery. The record was
reviewed, and Major Reno was reburied at the battlefield on 9 Sept. 1967 (New
York Times, 10 Sept. 1967, sec. 1: 41).

Works Cited

Brininstool, E. A. Troopers with Custer: Historic Events of the Battle of the
    Little Big Horn. Rev. ed. Harrisburg, PA: Stackpole, 1952.

Custer, Elizabeth B. Tenting on the Plains or General Custer in Kansas and
    Texas. New York, 1887.

"Custer, George Armstrong." Dictionary of American Biography. 1930.

Dellenbaugh, Frederick S. George Armstrong Custer. New York: Macmillan, 1917.

Fenin, George N., and William K. Everson. The Western from Silents to the
    Seventies. Rev. ed. New York: Grossman, 1973.

Frost, Lawrence A. Custer Legends. Bowling Green: Bowling Green U
    Popular P, 1981.

Graham, W. A. The Custer Myth: A Source Book of Custeriana. Harrisburg,
    PA: Stackpole, 1953.

- - -. The Story of the Little Big Horn: Custer's Last Fight. Harrisburg,
    PA: Military Service, 1952.

Holbrook, Stewart H. "Phonies of the Old West." American Mercury Feb. 1949:
    230-35.

Hunt, Frazier. Custer, the Last of the Cavaliers. Illus. Captain John W.
    Thomason. New York: Cosmopolitan, 1928.

Luce, Edward S., and Evelyn S. Luce. Custer Battlefield National Monument,
    Montana. National Park Service Historical Handbook Series. Washington,
    DC: National Park Service, 1952.

Miller, David Humphreys. Custer's Fall: The Indian Side of the Story. New
    York: Duell, 1957.

Montana. American Guide Series. New York: Hastings House, 1949.

New York Times 10 Sept. 1967, sec. 1: 41.

Stevenson, Burton E., ed. _Poems of American History_. Rev. ed. Boston: Houghton, 1922.

Stewart, Edgar I. _Custer's Luck_. Norman: U of Oklahoma P, 1966.

Utley, Robert M. _Custer and the Great Controversy: Origin and Development of a Legend_. Great West and Indian Series. Los Angeles: Westernlore, 1962.

Whittaker, Frederick. _A Complete Life of Gen. George A. Custer_. New York, 1876.

INDEX